*To M*

*Be coming Self Powered*

*Love*

*D13 2026*

SelfPowerment

To Megan

# ENDORSEMENTS

Deb Smallwood just *gets it,* and she shares it beautifully in *SelfPowerment.* She has a rare ability to understand the quiet struggles behind success and speak directly to what high-achieving women need to truly thrive in both life and business. As a high achiever myself—an attorney who recently returned to grad school to earn a master's from Harvard, as well as a coach, speaker, university lecturer, and mental health professional—I found true kinship in the stories Deb tells. Her framework with its four principles is refreshingly simple, profoundly effective, and filled with "aha" moments that stop you in your tracks. *SelfPowerment* is now my go-to recommendation for clients and colleagues alike.

**Kelly Greene, JD, ALM**
Center for Holistic Resilience

Having experienced first-hand the challenges of the corporate climb, and now as an executive coach to high-achieving women, I know how often success comes at the cost of self. I've sat at the boardroom table, navigated the unspoken rules, and coached women through seasons of burnout, transition, and quiet self-doubt masked by accomplishment.

What's missing for so many is a toolkit—not just for performance, but for presence. That's what *SelfPowerment* offers. It gives women the language, structure, and permission to know themselves deeply, to honor their strengths, and to access the inner clarity that true leadership requires. This isn't a book of theory—it's a guidebook for women who are ready to lead from the inside out.

**Jennifer Buras**
Senior Partner: Essex/Keystone Partners
Board Member: Hometown Financial Group, North Shore Bank, The YMCA of the North Shore (Past Chair), and Saint John's Prep

Having served as a CEO and global executive across some of the world's most influential organizations, I know what it takes for women to lead in complex, high-stakes environments. What often gets overlooked—but is essential—is the inner journey: the courage to reclaim your voice, owning your choices, and leading with authenticity rather than conformity.

*SelfPowerment* gives women permission not to ask permission. It's about rising into who you truly are. Deb is not giving us a lecture of how we should be but providing a roadmap from the vision of me to reality and execution. Deb's work meets women exactly where they are—at the intersection of ambition and alignment, logic and intuition, leadership and humanity. Whether you're in the boardroom or navigating your next chapter, this book is actionable, heartfelt, and deeply empowering.

**Karen T. Cone**
Corporate Board Directors and Venture Partner
Former CEO and Global Senior Executive
at IBM, Gartner, Mastercard, TowerGroup, Microsoft, and Mastersfund

As a first-generation immigrant, I know what it means to show up without the playbook—navigating a new country, new culture, and a business world full of unspoken rules. You learn to decode systems, push through discomfort, and figure it out on the fly. But what I've learned—often the hard way—is that success isn't just about strategy or grit. It's also about inner alignment.

That's why *SelfPowerment* spoke to me so deeply. It's not just a framework—it's a guide for women who are ready to lead from within. For immigrant women, for first-generation professionals, for anyone who's had to translate more than language to belong, this book is a compass. It reminds us that our power isn't in fitting in—it's in showing up fully, with clarity, stillness, and choice. Every woman navigating both ambition and identity needs this book in her corner.

**Lotti Siniscalco**
Partner: Emergence Capital
Board Member: Federato.AI, Method Fi, and Casap

*SelfPowerment* offers a practical guide for women who take leadership seriously and want to grow with purpose. Deb Smallwood provides strong, focused tools that help align values with action and support clear, confident decision making. As CEO of a property and casualty insurance company with over one billion dollars in annual premium, I value her emphasis on clarity, choice and personal accountability—qualities that define strong leadership.

**Gina Hardy**, CPCU, CIC, CRM, AIC, ARM, AMIM
General Manager and Chief Executive Officer
North Carolina Insurance Underwriting Association

*SelfPowerment* is a transformational guide for high-achieving women who want to create success from the inside out. As a leadership consultant, I've worked with countless women navigating the tension between high performance and personal alignment. Deb Smallwood doesn't just understand this tension—she offers a clear, compassionate framework for moving through it. This book is full of insight, heart, and powerful reminders that we don't need to strive our way into success—we can lead from who we already are. *SelfPowerment* is not just a guide—it's a gift.

**Susie Albert Miller**, MA, MDiv
Leadership and Communication Strategist, Speaker, and Author
*Listen, Learn, Love*

For any career woman who has wondered if there's more to life than a bigger role, a better salary, or a seat in the boardroom, *SelfPowerment* will help her achieve clarity of purpose, alignment with her passion, and a more personalized path to prosperity. With its unique roadmap for determining what truly matters, this engaging and enjoyable book will help women live and lead on their own terms, declaring, "Who I am is enough."

**Janet Switzer**
*New York Times* Bestselling Coauthor with Jack Canfield
*The Success Principles: How to Get from Where You Are to Where You Want to Be*

Working with graduate-level business students, I see every day how launching or shifting a career is as much an inner journey as it is a professional one. Technical skills and industry knowledge are important, but the ability to stay grounded, resilient, and authentic through change is what truly sets people apart.

*SelfPowerment* gives readers the tools to do exactly that. The four principles and eight strategies offer a clear, actionable framework for navigating uncertainty, making intentional choices, and aligning actions with personal values. It's practical without being prescriptive—equally valuable for a student stepping into their first role, a professional reinventing themselves mid-career, or anyone seeking more purpose in their work.

In a world where change is constant, *SelfPowerment* is a tactical guide to building the kind of inner strength that lasts a lifetime.

**Laurissa Berk, MS**
Director: Global & Experiential Education
School of Business, MS STEM Programs, University of Connecticut

# SELFPOWERMENT

The Inner Shift for High-Achieving Women
Who Want More than Just Success

## DEB SMALLWOOD

NEW YORK

LONDON • NASHVILLE • MELBOURNE • VANCOUVER • BOSTON

# SELFPOWERMENT

The Inner Shift for High-Achieving Women Who Want More than Just Success

Published in New York, New York, by Morgan James Publishing. Morgan James is a trademark of Morgan James, LLC. www.MorganJamesPublishing.com

Proudly distributed by Publishers Group West®

A **FREE** ebook edition is available for you or a friend with the purchase of this print book.

_____

CLEARLY SIGN YOUR NAME ABOVE

**Instructions to claim your free ebook edition:**
1. Visit MorganJamesBOGO.com
2. Sign your name CLEARLY in the space above
3. Complete the form and submit a photo of this entire page
4. You or your friend can download the ebook to your preferred device

ISBN 9781636989983 paperback
ISBN 9781636989990 ebook
Library of Congress Control Number:
2025947032

**Cover Design:**
Chris Treccani

**Illustrations:**
Kristen McCall

with...

Morgan James is a proud partner of Habitat for Humanity Peninsula and Greater Williamsburg. Partners in building since 2006.

Get involved today! Visit: www.morgan-james-publishing.com/giving-back

## DEDICATION

To my mother,
who broke cycles and showed me the power of inner strength.
For your courage and the gift of unconditional love,
I am forever grateful.

# DISCLAIMER

This book is for informational and reflective purposes only. It is not business, psychological, medical, or mental health advice, nor a substitute for professional guidance. Readers should seek qualified experts for matters specific to their personal or professional lives.

The content reflects the author's personal and professional experiences and collective insights. Stories are told as she remembers them—through her lens, in her words, and with the meaning they hold for her. While every effort was made to represent events truthfully, memory is imperfect, and some details may have shifted over time.

The book includes real-life case studies and research examples. All references to individual names, family members, company names, and other identifiers have been changed or disguised to protect privacy. In some cases, composite characters blend the experiences of multiple individuals, preserving the integrity of key themes while ensuring confidentiality.

Artificial intelligence (AI) was used for idea generation, transcript analysis, and content organization. AI served only as a support tool; all concepts, research, frameworks, and final content are solely the author's work.

The *SelfPowerment* Framework and all related tools are the exclusive property of Deb M. Smallwood LLC and are protected under US copyright laws. The *SelfPowerment* intellectual property remains solely owned by Deb M. Smallwood LLC. Unauthorized use, reproduction, or distribution of the *SelfPowerment* Framework or its related tools is strictly prohibited.

# TABLE OF CONTENTS

# FOREWORD

I've spent most of my life in the business world—coaching, advising, and working with leaders who want to create something meaningful. I understand what it takes to succeed. I also understand the toll it can take, especially for women who are juggling multiple roles.

We're not just professionals: We're partners, mothers, daughters, caregivers, volunteers, and mentors. And many of us strive to be excellent in every one of those roles, holding ourselves to impossibly high standards.

The pressure to perform can be relentless. And even when we rise to meet every demand, we're often left wondering why it still doesn't feel like enough—why, despite doing everything right, we feel so far from ourselves.

We don't talk about it much. Not out loud. But many high-achieving women live with a low hum of discontent. It's not failure that brings them to this moment—it's success. We've reached the top of our fields, ticked every box, and met every demand. And still, something feels off. Like somewhere along the way, we've drifted from ourselves.

That's the moment *SelfPowerment* speaks to.

This book isn't about burnout, though many women will see their own burnout here. It's not about starting over, though it may stir a desire for change. It's about waking up. It's about remembering that your power doesn't lie in how much you do, but in how deeply you live connected with who you really are.

And that's why I believe in this message so deeply.

I've felt that same inner restlessness, the questions that come after the goals are met. I've wrestled with the quiet sense that something more meaningful was calling me forward. Not something louder or busier, but something more true. And over time, I've learned that real fulfillment isn't about doing more. It's about coming back to what matters most.

This is where Deb Smallwood's voice is both steady and hard-won.

She has lived this transformation herself. She knows the masks we wear, the pressures we carry, and the grind that comes with high-level leadership. As a former technology executive and a widely respected thought leader, she isn't speaking from the sidelines. She's walked the very path she's now illuminating.

Deb has created something rare: a framework that is both deeply personal and widely relevant. She offers research without preaching, insight without pretense, and structure without rigidity. What she's created here is more than a method; it's an invitation. A way back to yourself.

And while yes, this book is full of strategy and practical takeaways, what moves me most is its humanity. The honesty, the compassion, and the courage to say, *You're not broken. You're waking up.*

But what makes her perspective so powerful isn't just her credentials; it's her wisdom. Deb brings language to what so many of us feel but haven't named. Her *SelfPowerment* Framework doesn't prescribe, it invites. It opens a door. She offers tools, stories, and truths that help you reconnect with your own sense of self and strength.

This is a book written by a woman who broke her own patterns. Who asked better questions. Who chose to become the kind of leader—and human being—she longed to be. And now, she's offering you the same path.

If something in you has been stirring, trust that.

Let this book meet you where you are and walk beside you as you examine what matters most. Not through striving. Not through perfection. But through reflection, inner honesty, and giving yourself much grace.

You don't have to walk away from your ambition. But it's time to bring yourself back to center.

You're about to step into a process of reflection and discovery that might change everything, not because it gives you all the answers, but because it helps you ask the right questions.

And along the way, you may start to see choices you didn't know you had, and realize that the life you've been craving has been within reach all along.

**Karen Anderson**

*Wall Street Journal* and *USA Today* Bestselling Author

*The Bezos Letters: 14 Principles to Grow Your Business Like Amazon*

# A NOTE FROM THE AUTHOR

For as long as I can remember, one simple phrase has carried me forward: *Why not me?*

Those three words became a quiet yet powerful challenge—a mindset that helped me navigate obstacles, seize opportunities, and silence doubt. *Why not me?* wasn't just a question; it was a declaration. A bold refusal to let barriers define me. A way of reminding myself that I was just as capable, just as worthy, just as powerful as anyone else in the room.

That question guided me through the ranks of corporate leadership and became the driving force behind decades of impact. I learned to use my voice, strategic insight, and passion for change to help companies grow and to help leaders lead. I climbed the ladder, broke a few ceilings, and reached what many would call the pinnacle of success.

The success? All true.

But along the way, although you would never know it by looking at me, I struggled (and trust me when I say, it wasn't always pretty).

Fortunately, I came through on the other side.

With hard work, determination, and the guidance of my family and some great executive coaches, I was able to realize what it meant to move from external achievement to inner alignment.

But I began to wonder: Was I the only one who wanted something more than just success?

As high-achieving women, we've reached nearly every corner of leadership—from the C-suite to boardrooms—but the numbers remain discouraging. And despite our progress, the statistics still paint a sobering picture. The barriers are still real. Sometimes, those barriers come from systems and expectations. But sometimes, they come from within, from old beliefs, inner doubts, and silent pressures we've carried for too long.

I had built a powerful career by asking, *Why not me?* But it was time to ask a different question: *Why not us?*

After years of helping organizations evolve, I wanted to help women succeed and thrive in the business world without having to go through what I, and so many women before me, had gone through. I wanted to help them reclaim their inner power. Not to become someone new, but to return to who they've always been beneath the noise.

I began to wonder: What if the insights, strategies, and hard-won wisdom I've gathered over the years could be used for more than just driving business results? What if they could help women lead lives of alignment, peace, and purpose?

That question brought me here, to this book.

What started as a simple research project quickly became a calling. I interviewed 52 high-achieving women leaders across industries (and included 10 men as a control group) to uncover what's really going on beneath the surface of success.

Through over 500 hours of research, recorded interviews, and analysis, I explored their stories, strategies, vulnerabilities, and wisdom.

What I discovered was profound: We don't need more tips for climbing faster and higher. We need new ways to live and lead from *within*. We need to connect ambition with authenticity. We need to lead with confidence rooted in inner peace. And we need each other to do it.

That is what *SelfPowerment* is. It's a mindset. A framework. A movement.

It's for the woman who is already successful but wants *more*. For the leader who knows how to perform but now wants to live and lead from a place of stillness, clarity, and choice.

It's for all of us who are ready to say: I don't need to prove myself anymore. I want to align my life and career with who I really am.

## How to Get the Most from This Book

I know how precious your time is. You're likely balancing a high-impact career, personal responsibilities, and the deep desire to keep growing without burning out. That's why this book is designed to be both inspiring and practical.

In the chapters that follow, you'll journey with me from ambition to alignment, from the pressure to prove to the freedom of inner peace. Along the way, you'll meet women who are living this inner shift—and explore a new kind of success that's grounded in purpose, not pressure.

Here's what you can expect …

In this first section, *The Journey*, I take you behind the scenes of my climb through the corporate world—rising to the top, leading large-scale transformations, and ultimately becoming CEO of a thriving strategic advisory firm. Again, on the surface, I was successful and by every external measure, I had made it.

But behind the scenes, the cracks were forming. I share the weight I carried, the moments of quiet doubt, and the growing sense that something essential was missing. What began as a relentless pursuit of achievement slowly gave way to a deeper kind of inquiry—one that would lead to an unexpected breakthrough and the start of a very different path forward.

The next section is all about *The Research*. You may ask: *Can I skip it?* Technically, yes—but I hope you won't. When I asked myself, *Was it just me?* I knew I had to dig deeper. I conducted in-depth qualitative interviews with high-achieving women to move beyond anecdotes and uncover meaningful patterns and data. What I discovered was powerful—and it just might surprise you.

The third section explores *The Framework*. From my lived experience and research, I developed four guiding principles that form the foundation of the *SelfPowerment* Framework, along with eight practical strategies you can begin using right away. (And it's my hope that you'll find the framework, with real stories and research insights, interesting, compelling, and relatable!)

You'll also get to know "Alex," a composite character based on real interviews, whose experiences bring these principles to life.

The final section, *The Inner Shift*, brings it all together. You'll see how to apply the framework, and the tools that go with it, in both your work and your everyday life. You'll also hear how other women have used these principles and strategies to create the kind of lives they truly wanted (but never felt they knew how or had time for).

Also in the final section—and one of my favorite parts—you'll hear from women leaders who are living *SelfPowerment* in real time. Their voices come from the research interviews, one-on-one mentoring, and the *SelfPowerment* Mastermind programs. Through their triumphs and challenges, they show what it truly means to put the principles into practice—with courage, clarity, and grace.

You might be wondering: Is this a business book, a career guide, or a personal development book? The truth is, it's all of those—woven into one.

But let's be clear—this isn't about walking away from your career or making impulsive decisions. It's about coming home to yourself. It's about remembering who you are beneath the titles, the striving, and the pressure to perform. It's about reclaiming your voice—not to shout louder, but to speak in a way that's true to you.

Do you have to read this book cover to cover in one sitting? Not at all. However, I would encourage you to read it straight through, as the principles and strategies build upon each other.

Although the *SelfPowerment* journey is designed to move through the principles in order, the framework is fluid. You can revisit it regularly as a tool to reset and realign. Depending on what you're facing, whether it's a new opportunity, a personal challenge, or a season of change, you may find yourself drawn more deeply into one principle than another. Wherever you are, that's the perfect place to begin. Come back to the strategies as needed.

Let the stories and reflection questions guide your discovery, spark insight, and support your growth.

*SelfPowerment* is for the woman who's done with the grind and ready to lead with clarity and intention. For the high achiever who knows how to succeed—but wants to feel aligned, not just accomplished. For the leader who's stopped asking, *What should I do?* and started asking, *Who am I, really?*

If that's you, you're right where you belong.

And as you move through these pages, I hope you'll feel something deeper: You're not in this journey alone.

But more than anything, I hope you remember what the world may have taught you to forget: Your greatest power was never outside of you. It's been within you all along.

Welcome to *SelfPowerment.*

# THE JOURNEY

# CHAPTER 1

# A Moment of Arrival

I was seated at the front of a chartered bus outside the Waldorf Astoria in New York City, dressed in a black sequined gown, my hair swept into a French twist, diamond earrings catching the light, and my signature red lipstick in place. Beside me sat my rock—Mark, my husband of 22 years—calm, proud, and handsome in his black tuxedo.

We were heading to celebrate one of the biggest milestones of my professional life: I had just been promoted to partner at KPMG.

When the senior partner stepped onto the bus and handed each of us a "passport" engraved with the KPMG logo, our destination was revealed: Ellis Island. The firm had rented the entire island for the new partner celebration.

I felt a wave of emotion rise.

All four of my grandparents had arrived through Ellis Island from northern Greece in the early 1900s. They came with little more than courage, a single suitcase, and the belief that a better life was possible. They didn't speak the language or know the culture. But they had grit. They had each other. And they had an unshakable determination to start something new.

Eventually, they would instill in their children and grandchildren that same determination to work hard, be resilient, and push forward. They taught us that family matters, that dignity matters, and that you do your best—*always*.

As I walked through those same doors they once walked through, I could feel their presence. I could almost hear them whispering the words to themselves, *Why not me?*

And they probably didn't call it this at the time, but I can imagine they had an affirmation they said to themselves in times of hardship: *You've got this.*

In that moment, I realized how far we had come.

Two generations earlier, women couldn't vote. They didn't have a voice in society, let alone a seat at the table. And now, here I was—walking the same worn floors they once stepped across, but in a gown and heels, celebrating my success as a partner in one of the world's most powerful professional firms.

I had built the life we all dreamed of—financial independence, a loving husband, two daughters, the house, the vacations, the title, the respect. On paper, I had it all.

But the truth was, I was exhausted and deeply unfulfilled.

Achieving partnership hadn't come easily. It came from years of grinding through fatigue and driving myself relentlessly to meet the impossible demands of my role. I wore my work ethic like armor. Every time I felt like I couldn't give any more, I'd push harder. *This is what you do to get ahead,* I told myself. *This is the price of success. This is the life we all want … isn't it?*

But inside, I was empty.

Each day felt like a performance, driven by relentless pressure and expectation. I became my title, feeding off the external success while quietly feeling more and more desperate inside.

I was working in an environment that didn't reflect who I was. KPMG was male-dominated and traditional, rooted in audit and tax. I, on the other hand, was a technology partner, so I often felt like an outsider, serving a system that didn't fully value or see me.

It wasn't intentional, but I stopped taking care of myself; there just wasn't time. I didn't exercise. I gained weight. I was living with daily anxiety and migraines. My thoughts were constantly spinning with self-doubt, fear, and frustration. Noise I couldn't silence.

I had reached what should have been the height of my success, but inside, I was running on empty. I was hitting every goal, checking every box. Yet something felt off. The spark that used to drive me was gone. I felt misaligned, weary, and unsure of how to move forward.

Because I not only did everything right, but I did it with excellence. I had become a human-*doing*.

Still, I convinced myself that I had arrived, and that was enough. That I loved the work, and I was where I was supposed to be. *After all*, I thought, *I'm meeting all the metrics. I'm doing everything right. This is what success looks like. There's no other choice, right?*

My life looked like success from the outside. But inside ...

I had lost myself.

## The Breaking Point

Eighteen months later, everything changed.

Following the tragic events of September 11, 2001, the business landscape in New York shifted dramatically, and KPMG decided to downsize its New York office.

In October, I was asked to resign as partner.

In the grand scheme of things, compared to the losses of 9/11, this was minor. But to me, it was devastating.

Despite consistently delivering some of the firm's highest results, I wasn't a certified public accountant. I was a technologist and the female partner who had championed me was no longer there. I wasn't part of the inner CPA network, and that made me vulnerable.

Despite my growing unhappiness and the toll it was taking on my health, leaving KPMG had never crossed my mind. After all, I had invested so much and worked so hard to get where I was. Walking away didn't feel like an option. Until it was forced on me.

With a mix of anger and embarrassment, I negotiated the terms and timing of my resignation, secured a solid severance package, and stepped away.

This wasn't just a professional blow; it cut to the core of who I thought I was.

Everything I had pushed toward for years suddenly fell out from under me. The loss of the title, the structure, and the role I had shaped my identity around left me feeling shaken and exposed.

For a while, I felt like I had let everyone down. My team. My family. Myself.

But I had been so committed to proving I belonged, to exceeding expectations, to fitting a mold that didn't match who I really was, that I had ignored the deeper truth: I hadn't been accountable to myself.

Looking back, I can see it now: KPMG was never truly my place. It was a respected firm and a good fit for many, but it wasn't aligned with my purpose, my powers, or my values. That misalignment between my role and my true self was like a slow leak, draining me from within.

But what felt like rejection at the time turned out to be a hidden blessing. It was a redirection—a turning point I couldn't have orchestrated on my own. Whether it was God, the universe, divine timing, or the whispers of my ancestors, something greater was guiding me toward what was next.

It turned out it wasn't the end. It was the beginning.

## Embracing Me

After I left KPMG, I knew I needed to restart, rebuild, and resurrect with confidence and self-worth. It was time to reset my professional compass and reconnect with who I truly was.

With the severance package, I invested in myself. I hired two exceptional executive coaches. This wasn't just about finding my next job; it was a journey of self-discovery. Together, we explored my innate strengths— my superpowers—and began connecting my future work with my true passions and abilities. It was no longer about chasing a title or fulfilling outside expectations. It was about building a career that truly reflected who I am.

As I peeled away layers of limiting beliefs, I began to shift my mind-set. I released the old narratives shaped by past experiences and started to see myself from a new perspective—capable, self-aware, and ready to lead from a place of clarity.

At the same time, I began taking better care of my physical health. I hired a personal trainer, began strength training, adopted a healthier diet, and reconnected with movement. I took up walking outdoors, playing golf, and going to the gym. It wasn't just about looking different. It was about reclaiming my energy and presence.

This integrated journey of self-care and discovery changed everything. When I eventually interviewed for a new role, I walked in fully confident, knowing the answer to the questions: Why me? And why them? I knew what I offered and why it mattered.

I landed an executive position at TowerGroup, a financial services advisory and research company. The transition felt natural. It allowed me to bring together everything I had built—my expertise in insurance, technology, and consulting—and to expand into new areas. I led research projects, wrote white papers, and advised clients with precision and ease.

I had found the right role at the right company, and I stepped into it unencumbered, settled in who I was, ready to grow even further.

### Unlocking Purpose Within

At TowerGroup, I was thriving in the traditional sense. I delivered strong results, led client work, and remained visible in the marketplace as a thought leader.

But on the inside, I was still stuck in high gear, still operating as a human-*doing*. My mind remained cluttered with noise: self-doubt, anxiety about the future, regrets from the past, and frustrations I couldn't control.

That's when I began working with a new executive coach who was unlike any I'd had before.

With a PhD in psychology and deep knowledge of Eastern wisdom and quantum physics, she guided me into a new way of thinking—one that included mindfulness, breathwork, living in the now, and gently letting go of the mental noise I had been carrying for years.

For the first time, I began to experience stillness—not just the absence of chaos, but presence. With a single breath, I could reset. With intention, I began to quiet the noise and reconnect with my inner being.

That space of stillness gave me something I hadn't had in years: peace.

I saw how much of my inner voice had been drowned out by external pressure and internal noise. As I deepened this breath practice, I reconnected with my intuition and inner wisdom. I began to hear what truly mattered, and it pointed me toward transformation and innovation, both professionally and personally.

This part of my journey marked a significant turning point. I wasn't just operating with confidence—I was grounded in who I was. I had unlocked a sense of purpose that came from within, not from achievement.

The door opened for something entirely new.

I was finally ready to step forward with purpose.

# CHAPTER 2

# The Inner Shift

The transformation that had started internally began to shape my outer world in meaningful ways. It was a turning point where everything began to reset, where I finally began living from a place of *being* rather than relentless *doing*.

At TowerGroup, besides producing results and hitting the numbers, I felt a sense of belonging I hadn't known before.

The CEO was one of the best leaders I'd worked with—supportive, strategic, and deeply committed to equity. She didn't just talk about fixing disparities; she took action. She adjusted salaries and corrected titles. Under her leadership, women were seen and valued.

The company's culture aligned with my values, and my role fit like a glove. As a research analyst and strategic advisor, I worked closely with C-level executives, leveraging my expertise in insurance and technology to capitalize on my strengths: integrating research, identifying trends, spotting patterns, and ultimately, guiding companies through transformational change.

Through it all, I continued working with my executive coach. That relationship taught me the most pivotal lesson of all about accountability. For most of my career, I had been accountable to everyone else—my team, my employer, my family. But I had neglected the one person I couldn't afford to ignore: me. (One of my few regrets is that I didn't realize that sooner.)

I realized that I had stayed at KPMG too long. No one forced me to remain in a role that drained me—I made that choice. I gave my power away by believing there wasn't another path. In the end, they decided for me, but I now understood I had always had the power to choose.

That realization cracked something open. I stopped trying to control every outcome and instead leaned into *presence*, simply focusing on the moment. I accepted what was, released the pressure, and made room for what would unfold. I trusted the process.

When I did, everything began to open up. All I had to do was look up and out. I began to see infinite possibilities I hadn't dared to imagine. With each act of surrender came a new kind of strength—strength that came from being able to choose.

I realized I was ready to leave behind what no longer served me and to create a company entirely of my own. Never in my wildest dreams had I imagined owning a company. I had been raised to pursue security—to find a good job and hold onto it. But something in me had shifted. I had clarity. I had courage. I had purpose.

And I acted on it.

Starting my own firm, which I called Strategy Meets Action, allowed me to integrate everything I had learned, everything I believed in, and everything I was becoming. It gave me space to lead, innovate, and serve in a way that felt fully integrated with who I was. I was working and living with passion, purpose, and joy.

I've never looked back. Creating Strategy Meets Action became one of the most liberating and fulfilling decisions of my life—both for me and for my family.

## Executive Presence from the Inside Out

As I began to move forward, alignment became the focus. I was determined to close the gap between who I was becoming and how I showed up in my work and life.

It was about reclaiming myself. Not tying who I was to a title or a résumé but allowing my true being to emerge and lead. It was about speaking with intention, honoring my own voice, and building relationships founded in integrity and purpose.

As founder and CEO, I wanted those values reflected in everything, from how we served clients to how the team treated each other. That required me to fully show up as myself, not the partner I once was, not the performer who had powered through, but the woman I had become. I had to stop letting roles define me and start letting my essence guide me.

This shift was subtle yet powerful. I was no longer just a human-*doing*—I was a human-*being* who was doing. And that changed everything.

This realization allowed me to reassess my professional identity. I had always worn many hats—operational, strategic, tactical, innovative—but now I saw that the hat didn't make the leader. My identity was rooted in something deeper, something unshakable.

I also became more aware of the voices I used in different spaces. I've always been great at execution. I could be direct, focused—a taskmaster. That voice had propelled me for years. Now, a new voice began to lead: the voice of the wise woman. It was calm, intuitive, rooted in stillness and insight. It helped me make better decisions and lead with strength and authenticity.

Stepping into another C-level role required me to integrate those voices. I had to (actually, wanted to) craft a new self-image—one of a leader, mentor, and visionary with a seat at any table. I leaned into transformation, both in the industry and within myself. And I brought others along for the journey, deepening my relationships and expanding my impact.

For 15 years, I led Strategy Meets Action with heart and purpose, building it into a multimillion-dollar national brand. The company thrived not only in business outcomes but also in culture, meaning, and reputation. I wasn't just successful; I was fulfilled.

Unexpectedly, in 2020, a venture-capital-backed global services firm, ReSource Pro, approached us. They saw our brand, our work, our clients, and our people, and they wanted to acquire us. The timing coincided with a rare stillness that had settled over the world during the pandemic. With fewer distractions, I had the mental space and emotional bandwidth to move forward with continued confidence and clarity.

Navigating due diligence and closing the acquisition was one of the most demanding chapters of my career, but I moved through it with the same internal compass that had guided me back to myself: clarity, stillness, choice, and intent.

Once again, I had created a better life. Not just for myself, but for my family and for the future I had dared to imagine.

## Reclaiming My Power Within

My journey of alignment didn't end with a title or the sale of my company. True *SelfPowerment*, I discovered, is a continual return to your center, especially in the face of life's daily pressures, transitions, and temptations to disconnect.

After selling Strategy Meets Action, I became an employee of the acquiring corporation, a large global services firm, as part of the buyout agreement. Almost immediately, I found myself drifting back into old patterns—chasing goals, running at full speed, performing instead of being. Once again, I became a human-*doing*.

My inner clarity began to blur. Exhaustion crept in. Frustration was on high alert. I was out of alignment. Toward the end of my second year of a three-year commitment, I started to question how I'd make it through another year.

Then came a pivotal dinner with my daughters (both accomplished women). As I shared my stress and frustration, they looked at me with love and challenge. "Mom, we love you," they said. "But we don't get it. What are you trying to prove? Why are you still there?"

My acquisition transition executive coaches had been asking me those same questions.

But that evening, my daughters reminded me of something I had taught them: the power of choice. Like Dorothy with her ruby slippers, I had always had the power to go home. I just had to decide to use it.

At first, I resisted what they were suggesting. After all, I had to fulfill the rest of my commitment. Plus, I was loyal to my clients and the team. But as my girls gently held space and asked the right questions, my clarity returned.

By the end of that night, I knew what I needed to do. I proposed a new arrangement to ReSource Pro: my final third year would be spent as a consultant. They agreed. (Sometimes, you just have to ask.)

I stepped away from running the daily operations and to a more flexible role to complete the acquisition transition focusing on client work. And just like that, the weight lifted.

I started walking early each morning at the golf course near our home, trying to find rhythm in nature, breathing deeply again. One morning, as my time at the company was coming to an end, a thought rose from within. It was simple, clear, and unmistakable: *I had done it again. I had lost my power.*

And then another thought followed: I always have a choice. I can choose to be *SelfPowered*.

Tears welled up. The word *SelfPowerment* had first come to me through an executive coach nearly two decades earlier. Now, it had a new meaning. A deeper resonance.

I decided to live *SelfPowered*. This was what "Deb 2.0" would be about.

As I finished out that third year, I got back to being the woman I knew I was.

That fall, I entered my next chapter. The path was clear: just as I had needed guidance to realign, so did other women. I wanted to show what it looked like to reclaim your power from the inside out.

I wanted to share the whole truth, not just the wins, but the weariness. Not just the milestones, but the misalignments. And how to get back to center when you get off-kilter. Because that happens to all of us from time to time.

After leaving the corporate world, I started to nurture new relationships and invest in deeper connections. I began mentoring a few women executives one-on-one. That grew to six. Then came workshops. Retreats. Masterminds. And the early foundation of what would become the *Self-Powerment* Framework.

As I listened to these women—smart, successful, driven—I realized they were wrestling with the same questions I had asked myself: *Is this all there is? Why am I not fulfilled? Why does this feel so heavy?*

So, I did what I've always done when a question takes hold. I got curious. I became the researcher again. I began interviewing other women, listening closely, seeking patterns and truths that went deeper than surface success.

And that's where this journey took a new turn.

What followed was a deep and illuminating exploration—one that began with a single, essential question:

*Where are we now?*

# THE RESEARCH

# CHAPTER 3

# The Research Project

We've come a long way ...

Women today are leading in every facet of business, science, education, medicine, engineering, and technology. We're running companies, solving global problems, shaping innovation, and breaking records. In many ways, we're living in a moment our mothers and grandmothers only dreamed of.

But we're not there yet.

In the United States, women still earn only 82 cents for every dollar earned by men.[1] And although more women than men graduate from college and earn advanced degrees, only 10% of Fortune 500 companies are run by women as of 2024.[2]

In the 2024 McKinsey & Company *Women in the Workplace* study, the 10-year report, it predicts that achieving gender parity is still 50 years away.[3]

Fifty years.

That puts full equity out to at least 2074, a year when many of our granddaughters will be nearing retirement. This is not acceptable.

Despite the progress we've made, the reality is that women still face persistent and complex challenges. Whether overt or subtle, we continue to hit glass ceilings, confront the "old boys' network," navigate broken rungs on the corporate ladder, and push back against deeply rooted generational bias and discrimination.

We can't afford to wait for the world to change for us.

Yes, the rules of engagement in business were built by men for men. That's reality.

But as high-achieving women, we must step into our own power, not only for ourselves, but for those who will follow us.

### Facing a Tenacious Opponent ...

While we continue to face challenges in corporate culture, often the biggest obstacle isn't external, it's internal.

The noise in our heads is loud. We become our own harshest critics.

Self-doubt creeps in, whispering that we're not enough. Feelings of inadequacy, impostor syndrome, and self-judgment rise quietly until they dominate.

Moments meant for growth become landmines we try to avoid. And eventually, the internal battle can leave us feeling paralyzed, exhausted, and disconnected from our true potential.

We begin to tread water, uncertain, unaligned, and unsure of how to fully reclaim our voice, our power, and our path.

How do we quiet the noise?

How do we awaken our powers and push forward?

I knew my own story. I knew the turning points, the breakthroughs, and the moments that shaped me. But I wanted to know more.

What about other women? How did they strive for success? Did they experience the same challenges? Were they also navigating the same inner conflicts and external pressures?

Were they discovering different strategies for resilience, alignment, and fulfillment?

So, I turned to my expertise as a strategic analyst and researcher. What began as a few conversations and small workshops quickly expanded into a full-scale research initiative, one that would surface trends, insights, and truths from women at the top of their fields.

The stories were powerful.

The patterns were undeniable.

And the findings were profound.

# CHAPTER 4

# The Methodology: Listening to High-Achieving Women

At my former company, Strategy Meets Action, I had led both formal qualitative and quantitative studies focused on strategy, technology trends, and digital transformation. That work sharpened my ability to identify patterns, gather meaningful data, and translate insights into action.

Now, as I shifted my focus to supporting high-performing women, I realized that this next stage needed to be grounded in the same research rigor. I wanted to go beyond anecdotal evidence and personal experience.

I needed something more robust to refine and solidify the *SelfPowerment* message—something that could deepen my understanding and validate the patterns I had sensed in conversations over the years.

The purpose of this research was threefold:

- To expand my knowledge beyond my personal journey and the informal insights I had gathered through 40+ years in the business world
- To understand the life and career journeys of other women
  - What made them successful?

- ○ How did they describe themselves in the workplace?
- ○ What came naturally to them, and what was hard as they climbed higher?
- ○ How did they define their most significant accomplishments?
- ○ And perhaps most importantly, were they truly happy and fulfilled in their careers?
- To give high-achieving women a platform to share their stories, many of whom, like me, had often felt unseen and unheard

With these goals in mind, I set out to identify common strengths, challenges, and strategies among women leaders and to capture the deeper emotional and personal context behind their success.

## Phase 1: Establishing Context Through Secondary Research

I began by immersing myself in masterclasses and podcasts hosted by business influencers across industries—both men and women—to gain a broader view of leadership trends and success factors.

Next, I conducted general secondary research to gather current statistics and explore how terms like authenticity, confidence, self-worth, self-doubt, impostor syndrome, and empowerment are commonly understood and used when discussing women in the workplace.

From there, I broadened my scope, studying notable women from around the world and across history. I went way back and began with Cleopatra, Olympias, and the Queen of Sheba, tracing a line through the last 200 years of American history to examine the lives and leadership of pioneering women in politics, business, invention, the arts, athletics, media, education, and activism.

I looked at spiritual teachers, authors, public figures, researchers, and elite performers. I sought to understand what made them stand out, what enabled them to challenge norms, and how they endured discrimination, cultural resistance, and setbacks.

Across these profiles, I identified nine traits these women consistently exhibited:

- Bold, strategic thinking
- Expertise and skill in their field
- Inner strength, courage, and confidence
- Integrity
- Living with intention
- Passion for their goals and beliefs
- Resilience and willingness to take risks
- Strong communication skills
- Personal accountability

These early findings shaped the development of my formal research approach. I moved into the next phase ready to explore more than just data—I wanted to listen deeply to the experiences of high-achieving women.

## Phase 2: Narrative Interviews and Firsthand Insight

The second phase of the project was formal, qualitative research guided by narrative inquiry methods. This means I used open-ended, story-driven interviews to explore lived experiences, values, emotions, and internal transformations.

Initially, I intended to conduct just a few interviews. But as the conversations began, it became clear this was something much bigger. The women I interviewed opened up in ways I had not expected. It was as though no one had ever asked them to share this deeply before.

They told stories from their childhoods, careers, and personal lives. They spoke of their accomplishments with pride, acknowledged the people who had mentored them, and reflected on the decisions that shaped their journeys.

Many also opened up about pain, both past and present. They talked about trauma from childhood, loss in adulthood, discrimination in the workplace, and the toll of pressure, performance, and burnout. They shared what made them feel powerful and what kept them up at night.

Some cried. Some expressed anger or fear. Several described the experience of being interviewed as "therapeutic." I felt deeply honored to hold space for these stories. Many offered to introduce me to other women they believed should be heard as well.

In total, I conducted interviews with 52 high-powered, high-performing women and 10 male leaders (a control group, if you will), all of whom self-identified as successful in their careers. More than 500 hours were dedicated to conducting interviews, analyzing data, and deep reflection.

## Research Demographics: Diverse Voices, Shared Ambition

The women and men in this study held advanced leadership titles, including CEOs, COOs, CFOs, CMOs, CSOs, CAOs, CCOs, CIOs, CTOs (yes, there are a lot of CXOs!), executive vice presidents, board members, partners, and directors.

They came from across the business spectrum and represented a wide range of industries:

- Insurance
- Banking and Global Payments
- Technology and Telecom
- Management Consulting and Outsourcing Services
- Healthcare and Life Sciences
- Startups, Venture Capital, Education, Hospitality, Research, Federal and State Government, Legal Services, Media, Defense Manufacturing, and Real Estate

To round out the industry representation, I also conducted secondary research on women in retail and consumer goods, entertainment, automotive manufacturing, and philanthropy. This gave further perspective on how leadership challenges and breakthroughs might differ by sector.

Their cultural and educational backgrounds were equally diverse. The women represented a rich tapestry of racial, ethnic, and cultural identities—including African American, Asian, Caribbean, European, Hispanic, Latin American, and American-born women of various heritages.

Some were immigrants or green card holders. Others traced their North American ancestry back for generations, including one whose family line reached the *Mayflower*.

Education levels varied widely. Some had no formal higher education. Others had graduated from local colleges or earned advanced degrees, including MBAs from top institutions such as Stanford, Harvard, Penn, and Brown. Several held law degrees, although none were practicing attorneys at the time of our interviews.

Generationally, the 52 women included:
- 8 baby boomers (age 60+)
- 27 from Gen X (age 45–59)
- 17 millennials (age 25–44)

The 10 male participants came from all three generations as well.

## From Insight to Illumination: What Comes Next

The conversations I had during this research were transformational—not just for me, but for many of the women I spoke with. Their stories were filled with depth, nuance, emotion, and wisdom.

While I expected to hear stories of success and perseverance, I was surprised by how many women chose to be deeply vulnerable. They did not just talk about what they achieved. They shared what they carried.

As I analyzed the data and reviewed the interviews, it became clear that several of the hypotheses I had started with were not entirely true. The journey of women in leadership is far more complex than a single story or strategy can capture.

These insights laid the foundation for the core of this book. What follows are the key themes that emerged from the research: patterns, truths, and challenges that consistently appeared across conversations, regardless of industry, background, or role.

These themes are the heartbeat of *SelfPowerment*.

They reveal not only how women lead and succeed, but what they're longing for. They offer a mirror for us to reflect on where we are, what we want, and how we can move forward—not just with ambition, but with alignment, clarity, and joy.

Let's explore the research and what it revealed.

# CHAPTER 5

# The Predictions and Findings

While some may find research boring, I actually find it fascinating. For me, understanding trends, patterns, and behavior is like a treasure hunt: what you find isn't always what you expect!

My original research hypothesis included five statements I wanted to validate. Much like my historical research in Phase I, I expected to find predictable results.

I did not.

**My Hypotheses**

**Hypothesis 1:** It has become easier to be a woman in the business world.

**Finding: Not true**

Discrimination, gender biases, and broken ladder rungs are still very real experiences.

When we look at the history of women in the workforce, the last 50 years have propelled women forward. After all, the glass ceiling has been broken; women are demonstrating success in every key C-suite role in most, if not all, industries.

Our modern, digital world with its 24/7 connectivity has created new challenges and expectations. And work and productivity are in front of us, anywhere and anytime. Post-COVID, a hybrid work environment creates complex challenges in managing careers, leading teams, navigating the social landscape, and managing office politics.

As baby boomer women, we painfully raised the bar for what's possible in business, and we did it. But we often paid a steep price in the form of burnout, personal sacrifice, and relentless pressure to prove ourselves.

Today, Gen X, millennial, and Gen Z women are questioning whether that cost is worth it. They're seeking success on their own terms, with a greater focus on balance, purpose, and well-being. Yet, many of the same challenges we faced while breaking ground in the 1980s and 1990s still persist, proving that the work of transformation is far from over.

Yes, new doors have opened for women in leadership. However, many struggles remain. Hybrid work and digital overload have added complexity, not ease. The climb may look different than it did for baby boomers, Gen X, and now millennial women, but it is not easier. It is simply a different type of hard.

* * *

**Hypothesis 2:** Successful women have a strong woman in their early life—during childhood, school, or early career—who modeled strength and power, showing that a girl or woman can be anyone and do anything.

**Finding: Partially true**
The hypothesis held true in some cases but not all. Nearly every woman interviewed recalled someone who inspired her and sparked her inner desire to pursue a career in business. Many reflected on the people who guided or encouraged them, who believed in their potential, and who reminded them not to be forgotten or overlooked. However, not everyone had a strong female role model who specifically showed them how to navigate and thrive in a male-dominated world.

For several participants, the person who modeled confidence or resilience was a man. Fathers and grandfathers were often cited as key figures who supported them early on. Teachers, coaches, or male mentors also played significant roles. In many cases, fathers were especially intentional about making sure their daughters could be financially independent and take care of themselves.

For others, that early influence did come from a woman—sometimes a mother or grandmother, but also aunts, cousins, or even a friend's mother. These women, whether they stayed at home or worked outside the home, embodied strength, courage, and resilience. They may not have held traditional leadership roles, but they demonstrated what it looked like to endure hardship, speak up, love their family, or live with integrity and purpose.

In summary, while many women were indeed influenced by strong female role models, others found their inspiration in male allies or less conventional sources. What was most consistent across the stories was that someone in their early life, regardless of gender or position, planted a seed of belief and showed them that they were capable of more.

\* \* \*

**Hypothesis 3:** Once they discovered their professional role, most leaders followed a linear path as they rose from one level to the next.

**Finding: Not true**
Although I expected some variation, the research clearly showed that very few women set out at the start of their careers with a specific end goal or a clear path to the roles they hold today. The hypothesis that most leaders advance in a straightforward, linear fashion was not supported.

While some began on traditional linear career tracks, most of these high-performing women experienced a shift. They were often tapped—either by someone within their organization or from outside—for bigger roles or high-impact strategic initiatives. These opportunities stretched them in new directions, requiring them to step beyond their initial areas of expertise. As a result, their career paths became less predictable and far more dynamic.

In reality, the majority of women followed nonlinear career journeys. These paths often crossed multiple business functions, industries, and even geographies, allowing them to grow, adapt, and advance in ways that a standard career ladder could not have anticipated. It was this blend of flexibility, opportunity, and adaptability that ultimately shaped their professional growth.

\* \* \*

**Hypothesis 4:** Women at the C-suite level have to be inauthentic to be successful.

**Finding: Not true**
While it's true that navigating a business world historically designed by and for men presents real challenges, the research did not support the idea that women must be inauthentic to succeed at the highest levels. In fact, many of the high-performing women interviewed were leading from a place of authenticity, grounded in a strong sense of self, confidence, and clear purpose.

These women had learned how to use the right voice in the right settings. They understood which battles were worth fighting and how to effectively operate within male-dominated environments. What may sometimes appear as inauthentic from the outside is actually strategic navigation—knowing how to "play the game" in a way that allows them to succeed without compromising who they are.

What emerged most clearly through these conversations was just how brilliant, strong, and resilient these women are. They bring diverse talents, skills, backgrounds, and ambitions to the table. They are reliable, adaptable, passionate—and often underestimated. But their resilience speaks volumes.

Authenticity, as it turns out, is not a liability. For these women, it's a strength.

\* \* \*

**Hypothesis 5:** High-achieving women have a relentless drive for success and fulfillment fueled by an external motivation, such as the desire to overcome barriers or break generational cycles to create a better future for themselves and their families.

**Finding: Partially true**

It's clear that every woman at this level is driven. They work hard, push through the grind, and are committed to achieving success. Initially, I expected most of this drive to come from external sources—similar to my own experience growing up alongside my sister. As daughters of a first-generation American mother, we were determined to build on what she had worked so hard to start. Like many, I wanted to continue carving out a better life for my family, just as my mother had done with such strength and courage.

What I discovered through the interviews, however, was a more complex picture. The motivation behind high achievement was a blend of both external and internal forces.

Most of the women were, in fact, breaking some kind of generational cycle. Many spoke openly about their desire to create a better life, not just for themselves, but for their children, families, and communities. For some, that external mission was the spark that ignited their ambition.

But just as often, the motivation came from within. A deep, internal drive—something embedded in who they are—pushed them forward. This inner fire wasn't dependent on outside validation. It came from their values, their vision, and their personal sense of purpose.

In the end, while external influences often shaped their path, it was the internal conviction, the relentless desire for both success and meaning, that sustained their momentum.

# CHAPTER 6

# The Takeaways

After months of research, interviews, and reflection, a powerful truth emerged: while each woman's path is deeply personal and distinct, there are common threads that quietly unite them.

This isn't about making conclusions—it's a distillation. A weaving together of themes that surfaced not just once, but again and again. These aren't just anecdotes or observations; they are lived experiences that reveal the complexity, brilliance, and challenges of being a high-achieving woman today.

There are stories of confidence and doubt, loyalty and exhaustion, barriers and breakthroughs. These takeaways highlight not only the personal choices each woman made, but also the systems they had to navigate and the mindsets they had to shift. They reveal the quiet tension between ambition and authenticity—and the clarity that comes when a woman begins to lead from within.

This chapter honors that paradox: women are unique, but they are also united by a shared strength that runs deeper than titles, résumés, or roles.

What follows is not meant to summarize the entire journey, but to shine a light on the essential truths that rose to the surface.

### Unique Yet United: The Diverse Fabric of Women's Strengths

Each woman has a unique combination of life experiences, circumstances, talents, skills, and beliefs, much like a personal DNA signature. Every story is different. Every woman is valuable. Despite this diversity, some common threads emerged:

- A deep love for family
- A strong work ethic
- A commitment to giving back
- A drive for independence

These shared attributes create a collective resilience and strength. When we embrace our uniqueness, we are able to live and give more authentically. (This is why a foundational section of the *SelfPowerment* Framework is devoted to discovering, celebrating, and knowing your whole self and your personal superpowers.)

Our human nature must become the compass that guides our choices and fulfills our purpose.

---

**RESEARCH SPOTLIGHT**

"You already have everything you need. It's not just about resilience—
it's about transformation and the clarity that comes from truly knowing yourself."

**~ Nikki | Chief Marketing Officer**

---

### Confidence Amidst Doubt: Navigating Self-Perception

Confidence and self-doubt often coexist in the lives of women leaders. Many of the women I interviewed showed outward confidence in their roles and abilities, but at the same time, internal doubt was common. It could be triggered by unclear expectations, past experiences, or the pressures of their environment.

Some executives had developed their own techniques or utilized tools to manage the mental noise. Others admitted that self-doubt could lead to paralysis. From my own experience with discrimination and a deep concern for others' opinions and judgment, I understand the weight of this struggle. The key is not eliminating self-doubt completely, but learning to notice it, pause, hold it, acknowledge it, and let it go before it takes over.

---

**RESEARCH SPOTLIGHT**

"Everyone has self-doubt—men, women, people with privilege, people without … Even third-generation venture capitalists have self-doubt! And if *they* have self-doubt, it's okay if *I* have it too. Even if I try to push it away, it's part of me. And the more I push it away, the more pressure it creates. So, just let it out, cry it out, ask for support. There's no point in hiding it."

**~ Sophia | Partner**

---

### The Power of Choice: Balancing Multiple Roles

Women leaders are intelligent, strong, and brave. They excel at prioritizing, compartmentalizing, and delegating tasks that are not essential. This helps them survive and thrive in demanding work environments. They are loyal and passionate, committed not only to their companies but also to their teams and families. However, this level of dedication often comes at a personal cost.

Many women shared that they put their own needs last, which led to physical, emotional, and mental exhaustion. One executive described the guilt she carried from trying to manage her work and family. At work, she felt bad for taking time for her family. At home, she felt bad for working long hours. No matter where she was, she feared being seen as weak if she could not do it all.

This story was echoed by many others. It is hard. Many millennials questioned whether this version of success is even worth it. The truth is, to thrive, women must become accountable to themselves. They must choose their own priorities and give themselves permission to do so.

Career decisions are personal. Before we can step fully into our power, we must first recognize our right to choose what is right for ourselves.

> **RESEARCH SPOTLIGHT**
>
> "I don't feel like there's pressure between my roles. That's probably because I look at my identity as a mother, wife, and businesswoman, and I just make time for it ... It's just about making time for those things that help you still feel motivated and driven."
>
> **~ Ann | Chief Executive Officer**

## Persistent Challenges in the Workplace: The Ongoing Battle

Despite decades of progress, many women continue to face significant barriers in the workplace. Discrimination, gender bias, stereotypes, and unequal compensation remain common. The glass ceiling still exists, and toxic workplace cultures continue to wear people down.

Many expressed being frustrated with workplace politics and the ever-present influence of the good old boys' network. One woman even said she knew she had a seat at certain leadership tables, but there were other tables she knew she wasn't invited to; they were invisible.

The women who lead with clarity and self-worth do not ignore these challenges. They experience them deeply but choose to navigate them with strategic awareness. Rather than get stuck in anger or regret, they focus on what they can influence. They lead with intention, take action when they can, and align their careers with their values.

These women are not just surviving, they are rising above it all. They are transforming companies, mentoring others, and driving transformational change within and around them.

> **RESEARCH SPOTLIGHT**
>
> "I definitely had to put up with some 'crap' along the way. But I never let it define me. I learned how to navigate the bias—how to stay true to myself while advancing in a system that wasn't built to support women."
>
> **~ Jade | Partner**

## Gender Dynamics in Business: Different Approaches, Same Goals

Men and women often approach leadership differently. Women typically tend to focus on collaboration, team development, and long-term problem-solving. Men, on the other hand, often lead with business results and their legacy in mind.

When addressing opportunities, men begin with the *why* and the *what*. Women often start by defining the problem (*what*) and the *how*.

This can result in women being perceived as more operational and less strategic, despite demonstrating strong emotional intelligence and often being highly effective.

Networking patterns also differ. Men network to position themselves for future roles or to gain business insights. But women tend to network for emotional support. Still, many feel reluctant to ask for help or leverage their connections for advancement. This can limit their opportunities and slow their career growth.

---

### RESEARCH SPOTLIGHT

"Women founders pitch differently than men. Men lead with the *why* and the *what*—big vision and bold claims. Women often focus on the *how*—strategy, execution, operational excellence. But then many male executives tune out. They don't recognize the value in the details that actually drive success."

**~ Sharon | Board Director & Retired Global Managing Director**

---

## The Burden of Proof: Working Harder for Recognition

A common story emerged among the women interviewed. Many felt the need to constantly prove their value by taking on additional responsibilities, including tasks that others avoided, as well as mentoring and supporting their teams. Despite these efforts, many were not rewarded with the recognition, titles, or compensation they had earned.

This behavior often stemmed from perceived impostor syndrome and the belief that their worth is tied to output. This mindset can lead to overwork, burnout, and self-neglect.

But to break this cycle, this mindset has to change.

It's not about working harder. And it's not just about investing in yourself, whether through continued education, building new skills, nurturing your well-being, or pursuing professional goals.

It's about believing in your worth and value. When your energy is directed inward, the result is increased confidence and meaningful impact.

---

**RESEARCH SPOTLIGHT**

"I started my career by taking on more and more—more responsibility, more people, more budget. But my title and compensation stayed the same. I had to fight for seven months just to receive what I had already earned."

**~ Morgan | Chief Operating Officer**

---

### Financial Security vs. Fulfillment: A Delicate Balance

Early in their careers, many women chased promotions, salaries, and titles as markers of success. Over time, however, the pressure to achieve drowned out their deeper purpose. The constant drive, to-do lists, and expectations left little time for reflection.

Few women paused long enough to ask, Why am I really here? or What matters most to me?

The answers were often buried under layers of ambition and the demands of daily life.

Some individuals stayed in roles that no longer served them, prioritizing financial security despite feeling overlooked or devalued. While some found fulfillment in their teams or work, others experienced toxic environments that negatively impacted their well-being. The result was often a quiet longing for something more meaningful.

A growing number of women are beginning to define success on their own terms. Some are choosing to step away from traditional paths before being "sunsetted," in search of work that brings both fulfillment and sustainability.

> **RESEARCH SPOTLIGHT**
>
> "I remember every week my father handing my mother the money that she could spend that week. That made a huge impact on me to the point where I said, *I am never going to be in that situation.* It wasn't that it was a negative situation between my parents—it was just an economic necessity. But I knew that I was going to have my own money. That decision was very impactful."
>
> **~ Lindsay | Executive Vice President**

## Women Helping Women: A Positive Connection

Historically, women have been insular within organizations and have not prioritized networking for career growth. As seen in *Gender Dynamics in Business*, men often use their networks for advancement and access, while women focus more on emotional support and personal guidance.

Additionally, many women juggle multiple roles at home as mothers, spouses, or caregivers, which leaves little time or energy to build strategic relationships.

The difference is significant.

While men often credited networks for their advancement and decisions, few women even mentioned external networks as part of their career stories. That gap must be addressed.

The good news is that things are changing. Many interviewees shared encouraging stories of mentorship, women-focused groups, and collaborative efforts that helped them grow. The culture of women supporting women is becoming stronger.

> **RESEARCH SPOTLIGHT**
>
> "We can't do this alone. The system wasn't built for us—so we need to build something better and do so *together.* A new way forward that supports where we want to go."
>
> **~ Sophia | Partner**

## An Unexpected Finding: The Hidden Thread of Suffering

One of the most profound and unexpected revelations from this research was the universal experience of pain and suffering shared by these highly accomplished women.

We all know, intellectually, that life can be hard. But after conducting 52 in-depth interviews, the sheer consistency of pain woven into nearly every woman's story was striking.

It didn't matter their background, title, or achievements—suffering showed up, again and again, in deeply personal ways. For many, it was tucked quietly beneath the surface of their success.

"Suffering" wasn't a word I had ever used to describe my own journey. I didn't initially think of my experiences in those terms. But as I listened to story after story, I began to see it in a different light. The truth is, pain is part of every person's background, whether spoken or unspoken.

Some women shared stories from childhood. Others spoke of hardship as adults—loss, betrayal, trauma, illness, or burnout. Some of their stories left me stunned. Others broke my heart. What they had endured, and still managed to achieve, was extraordinary.

And it wasn't only those who came from difficult or disadvantaged circumstances. Even women who, by today's standards, would be considered to have lived privileged lives shared stories of deep, ongoing pain. The sources were different, but the emotional reality was the same.

For some, their pain became a catalyst, fueling resilience, shaping purpose, and pushing them to achieve. For others, it created a weight they still carry, sometimes holding them back in ways they are still trying to understand.

This insight changed me.

It reminded me that we never truly know someone's story by looking at their title, résumé, or even how they show up in a room. We don't know what she has survived, what she's facing, or what she's quietly holding together.

That's why compassion matters. That's why kindness is essential. And that's why, as women, we must stop judging and start helping—without comparison, without assumption, and without hesitation.

Because behind every strong woman is often a story of silent struggle. And when we see that, we begin to lead differently—with empathy, respect, and the understanding that strength and suffering often walk hand in hand.

## Digging Deeper

As I evaluated the research findings, I felt compelled to delve further. I wanted to understand not just what these women had accomplished, but *how* they had become who they are, and *why* their paths took the shape they did.

So, I returned to the transcripts with fresh eyes, asking questions like:

- What did these women have in common, despite their diversity of background, industry, and life experience?
- Why did some rise with visible confidence and strength, and how did they stay authentic in environments that often reward conformity?
- What helped shape their journeys—the key influences, defining moments, and setbacks they had to overcome?
- Why did so many feel trapped or paralyzed by the noise in their own heads, despite their undeniable accomplishments?
- And most importantly, what was different about those who were not just surviving—but thriving—with peace, confidence, and joy?

Each of the women I interviewed had achieved something remarkable in her career. They were highly skilled, focused, and driven. They demonstrated an inner clarity and resilience that set them apart.

But they had also faced profound internal struggles. At some point in their journey, all of them encountered self-doubt. The difference was that many had learned how to manage it—how to acknowledge it without letting it take over.

They had discovered their "superpowers," and along the way, they realized something powerful: they always had the ability to choose—how to lead, how to live, and how to move forward.

Most were clear: nothing about their path had been easy. Every step took grit, intentionality, and effort.

But they wouldn't trade it. They saw the value in the struggle. They owned their stories.

A few women shared that they had developed an inner connection with their being through spiritual or grounding practices such as prayer, religion, chanting, breathwork, yoga, or meditation. These practices were usually done privately, often at home or in a safe, personal space.

Surprisingly, very few brought that part of inner self into their professional environments. Even those who held deep spiritual or religious beliefs tended to compartmentalize that aspect of their lives—leaving it behind at the office door. As a result, they missed the opportunity to bring their full humanity—their full being and full power—into the workplace.

When asked to reflect on their journeys, none of the women expressed regret. But many shared a similar refrain: I wish I had learned some things earlier.

They wished they had known how to use their voice effectively, how to choose which battles to fight, how to network not just broadly but strategically. Several said they wished they had felt more confident asking for help without guilt or hesitation. Others admitted they had misunderstood the idea of balance. They now saw that work–life balance is really about conscious choices and clear priorities—not a perfect split, but intentional alignment.

A few expressed the desire to have gone further, to higher roles, bigger platforms. Some wished they had pursued advanced degrees such as an MBA, CPA, or law degree. But even in those reflections, their tone was not regretful. It was thoughtful. These were lessons gained through lived experience.

The women who were thriving had something in common. They had stopped trying to succeed by mimicking men. They had found the courage to speak up, take risks, and lead from their true center. They prioritized self-care, not as an indulgence, but as a requirement. Physical, mental, and emotional wellness weren't optional. It was essential to their ability to perform, lead, and sustain impact.

In the end, powerful themes emerged from the research and together, they reflect the strength, wisdom, and beauty that women bring to leadership when they choose to lead from within—fully, unapologetically, and in alignment with who they really are.

# CHAPTER 7

# The Patterns and Possibilities

The stories, insights, and experiences shared by the women (and men) I interviewed were a gift. I am beyond grateful for their willingness to open their hearts and give their time. Their reflections not only enriched my life, but they also deepened my understanding of what it truly means to be a woman in leadership today. Their words, shared in their own voice, revealed more than just individual journeys, they uncovered a shared truth.

One thing became abundantly clear: it is still significantly difficult for women in the workplace.

Despite progress, the cost of success remains high. The old models of achievement, relentless drive, constant proving, and the sacrifice of well-being are no longer sustainable. Yes, success is possible. A few of the women I spoke with have discovered how to tap into their inner being and honor their human powers. They experience peace, joy, and fulfillment in the midst of their professional accomplishments. But for many others, success has come at a steep price—burnout, disconnection, exhaustion, and a growing sense that something essential is missing.

Again and again, I heard women share that they were making unexpected choices. Some were stepping away from the executive track. Others were leaving the corporate world earlier than planned. Many were reinventing themselves through consulting, entrepreneurship, or fractional leadership roles. These were not decisions born from failure or lack of ambition. They came from a deeper place, a knowing that external success alone is not enough.

What emerged was a powerful theme: a longing not just to achieve, but to align.

These women were no longer chasing titles or promotions. They were seeking truth, purpose, peace, and freedom. They were waking up to a deeper shift, one that redefined success not by outward recognition, but by how they felt in their lives. They wanted success without regret, confidence without ego, and impact without depletion. They were no longer willing to postpone joy.

They are not giving up. They are rising differently.

As I reflected on the research, I saw my own experience mirrored in their stories. Through mentoring 12 women leaders and facilitating multiple mastermind workshops, I had already begun to witness this shift. The findings only confirmed what I had been observing for years and living myself.

This realization became the fuel for a new mission: to create a clear, practical, and deeply transformational guide that empowers women to reconnect with their inner strength, embrace their full human-*being*, and thrive not just in their work, but in every area of life.

**Stepping into a New Way**

We are at a tipping point. A new way of being in the business world is not only possible, it is necessary.

Across industries, I met women who are doing it differently. They have learned to quiet the mental noise, to trust their inner voice, and to lead with clarity and purpose. These women are not chasing someone else's definition of success. They are aligned with their own.

What they've discovered is available to all of us. There are specific patterns, principles, and strategies that lead not only to achievement, but to lasting fulfillment, peace, and joy. We do not need to sacrifice ourselves to succeed. We do not need to burn out to prove our worth. We do not need to compromise our values or silence our truth.

We need a new framework. One that honors our full humanity, restores our joy, and aligns our lives and careers with what truly matters.

The question now becomes: *How?*

- How do we awaken our strength and power within?
- How do we lead and live with clarity and confidence?
- How do we stay aligned in the middle of life's demands?

That is what the *SelfPowerment* Framework is designed to answer.

Through four core principles, you'll discover a roadmap to help you return to your center to live and lead from the inside out.

You'll also explore eight strategies that bring these principles to life.

These tools are not tasks to complete, but pathways to alignment and transformation. They are flexible, adaptable, and responsive to the real world we live in.

Even if you feel strong in one area or need to recalibrate in another, this framework will guide you back to yourself. It is not about doing more. It is about being more—more present, more grounded, more whole.

The challenges for high-performing, high-achieving women are real. So is the opportunity. You can achieve and thrive. You can be successful and fulfilled.

Whether you are …

- a woman who has achieved career success but feels exhausted, stuck, or unfulfilled,
- someone who has reached their goals but longs for something more meaningful,
- someone who has experienced a recent event that has shaken you, leaving you feeling lost and without a path forward, or
- a woman simply ready to align your life and career with who you truly are,

... the *SelfPowerment* Framework is for you.

This is the moment for a new approach—one that is more aligned, more intentional, and more life-giving. It is time to shift. To honor your inner strength. To live and lead with clarity, peace, and purpose.

It is time for *SelfPowerment*.

# THE FRAMEWORK

# CHAPTER 8

# The Foundation of *SelfPowerment*

"You alone are enough."
~ **Maya Angelou**

Sometimes, the most pivotal moments in life happen at the most ordinary times. For me, this occurred early in my career during a Myers-Briggs leadership training session.

I had just stepped into a new role as an information technology (IT) manager at Liberty Mutual and was hoping to better understand my leadership style. The trainer asked a question I had never been asked before—one that reshaped how I understood leadership, self-discovery, and the power of knowing my strengths.

*"If you opened your front door and saw an elephant standing there, what would you do?"*

(Take a moment to consider that question for yourself: If you opened your front door and saw an elephant, what would *you* do?)

My instinctive response was immediate. "Ride it, then sell it." It made perfect sense to me. I saw it as a challenge to tackle and a valuable opportunity.

What surprised me was how others answered. Some said they'd call for help. Others suggested they'd shelter and feed it.

Since this was a leadership training session, I couldn't help but wonder how those whose first instinct was to nurture the elephant would get their team to execute, meet deadlines, or achieve performance goals.

Looking back, my response perfectly reflected the leadership style I had embraced in those early years: action-oriented, strategic, results-driven. I valued strength, intelligence, and determination, characteristics fitting of an elephant. I believed I could accomplish anything through grit, drive, and hard work. Plus, I was convinced *my* way was the only way.

But the truth is, I was missing something.

My approach lacked gentleness. I didn't yet value emotional intelligence, relational awareness, or the power of intuition. I couldn't yet see that those, too, were forms of strength.

It would take me another two decades to fully understand the power of different leadership styles and the importance of balancing them within myself.

To this day, the elephant question still resonates. It wasn't just an icebreaker. It became a lens—a way to explore how people see the world, how they approach challenges, and how they take hold of opportunities.

When I conducted interviews for the *SelfPowerment* research, I included that same question. The answers were just as diverse and insightful as the women themselves:

- Some said they would run.
- Others would stand in awe, taking in the moment.
- A few said they'd find shelter, food, or water for the elephant.
- Some imagined using the elephant's strength to move heavy things.
- And yes, a few—like me—said they'd ride it.

Each answer revealed something profound about how these women instinctively move through the world, offering a glimpse into their unique strengths. It reminded me that there is no single "right" way to lead or live.

Just as there are many valid responses to finding an elephant at your door, there are many valid ways to be successful, fulfilled, and powerful.

Your authentic self, your human-*being* is your greatest strength. It's where your inner power begins.

And your greatest power is the choice to work and live in alignment with that truth.

## What Defines You?

In the rush of ambition and daily responsibility, it's all too easy to lose touch with your inner power. You start to believe your value is found only in what you do. Your title becomes your identity. Your accomplishments become your worth.

But those external markers miss something critical. When you're defined by your tasks, activities, and just plain *doing*, it only takes one crisis, one unexpected change, or one harsh evaluation to knock you off center. Confidence unravels. Clarity fades. Strength turns to stress.

Maya Angelou's words remind us, though, "You alone are enough."[4]

When you believe that, when you know that your value is already inside you, you can stop chasing approval and start choosing alignment. You can recognize your voice, your perspective, and your presence as valuable. You can stop trying to measure up to someone else's version of success.

Your self-worth isn't tied to titles, accolades, or comparisons; it comes from within.

You no longer need to meet impossible standards and expectations set by others. You no longer need to wait for validation.

You already are enough.

And unlike empowerment, which suggests that external power is given to you by someone else, *SelfPowerment* is about unlocking the power that already exists within you.

In other words: you don't need permission—you already have it.

This is the heart of *SelfPowerment*.

## The *SelfPowerment* Framework

Frameworks have always been my go-to tool for simplifying complex concepts. They allow me to break down intricate ideas and visually illustrate relationships. They help make sense of the *why* and the *what.* They aid in aligning guiding principles with real-life stories, and they turn ideas into practical how-to guides for change. Frameworks make learning digestible, actionable, and impactful.

So, when the idea of *SelfPowerment* began to take shape, I knew it needed a framework.

But not just any framework.

This one had to reflect the whole person—it had to be dynamic, dimensional, and deeply personal to support high-achieving women on a transformational journey that goes far beyond external achievement.

Most leadership models focus on what you do, your strengths, your leadership style, and your approaches to achieve measurable results. Very few begin with who you are, the awakening of your presence—your consciousness, breath, and unique human qualities and attributes.

So, unlike traditional leadership models, the *SelfPowerment* Framework integrates both Eastern and Western teachings and approaches. It blends spiritual principles with practical tools designed for the business world.

Rather than starting with the *why* and *what, SelfPowerment* starts with the *who*—truly knowing who you are.

That's why the *SelfPowerment* Framework is different.

And at the center of this framework lies its most essential element: *"I am ..."*

## The Center of the Framework

When I first discovered my inner power—something that could not only shift my mindset but also transform my career and my life—I found a feeling of joy and peace I didn't know was possible, a feeling of bliss I had never experienced.

That feeling didn't come from a title, a paycheck, or a promotion. It came from *within.*

With that, I realized I had been a human-*doing.* I had lost my *being,* the essence of who I was. That was a huge aha!

*"I am ..."* is at the core of my identity and yours—the always-present, unchanging self that exists beneath the surface of all the roles, labels, and expectations we've picked up over the years.

"I am ... my breath."

"I am ... my energy."

"I am ... my being."

This simple yet profound statement became the foundation of *Self-Powerment.*

## A Human-*Being*, Doing

Placing *"I am ... "* at the center of this framework invites you to focus on being *before* doing.

It's about recognizing who you wholly are, your physical body, your beautiful mind, your inner landscape, before identifying with what you do. You are a human-*being*, first. Then you can become a human-*being*, doing. A concept I learned from various books and teachings by Eckhart Tolle, "You are a human being, not a human doing."[5]

This is the fundamental shift that happens within *SelfPowerment.* When you know and embrace your *"I am ...,"* you can begin to align your actions with who you are and move with greater ease, confidence, and clarity.

Your *"I am ..."* is your anchor. It's where you find grounding, strength, and direction.

## Using *"I Am ..."* as Your Anchor

Whether you see your *being* as a divine gift from God, the universe, or another spiritual source, this belief in your value and uniqueness is what activates qualities like self-love, self-sufficiency, self-worth, and self-expression.

These attributes aren't external—they're born from within. They are the building blocks of a life that is both successful and fulfilling. When you know and love your *"I am ...",* you unlock and reclaim the ability to live your life with joy and impact. It becomes the spark of your transformation and the compass for your decisions.

You are a human-*being* before you are *doing*. That is where the inner shift begins.

## Owning Your Choices

This journey is not just about career growth or personal achievement. It's about choosing a mindset that allows you to live with ease, tap into all of your human and inner power, and have a new feeling of success.

Too often, we wait for others to give us permission to validate our dreams, our ambitions, or our next steps. We hesitate, hoping for the perfect opportunity or affirmation from someone else. But no one else can live your life for you.

Eckhart Tolle said it best: "You are the only one who can live your life. No one else can do it for you."[6]

When you stand in your human-*being*, you must also take responsibility for your *doing*. You are the only one who can walk your path, make your choices, and live your life with intention.

So today, I invite you to stand in your *"I am ... "* Let it be your declaration of existence, power, and potential.

## Living It Out

Take a moment to pause and reflect. Begin naming your *"I am ... "* statements to distinguish your *being* from your *doing*. (Don't worry about perfection—this is just your first draft. You'll return to it again as we move through the principles of the framework.) Let this be your reorientation to the truth of who you are: your breath, your energy, your unique and powerful essence.

Next, make Eckhart Tolle's quote your own:

"I am the only one who can live my life. No one else can do it for me."

This is your choice. So simple, and yet so powerful.

\* \* \*

You, wise and wonderful woman, are enough. Your being is worthy. You are deserving of a successful career and a deeply fulfilling life—one filled with peace, joy, and purpose. Your strengths, your perspective, your experiences—everything about you—are part of the incredible power within.

# CHAPTER 9

# The Framework as Your Guide

In the chapters that follow, we'll explore the four key principles that help you tap into your power within, along with eight strategies that offer practical tools to put those principles into action.

Each principle serves as a checkpoint—an invitation to pause, reflect, and realign—no matter where you are in your journey or what season you are in.

This work is about more than achieving personal or professional success. It's about inner transformation. It's about flourishing your human-*being* with peace, passion, and a new feeling of fulfillment in every area of your life.

Living *SelfPowered* means adopting a mindset that prioritizes inner peace, embraces ease, and fuels a positive impact in your world. It is a mindset shift that leads to sustainable, meaningful success.

It is also a form of liberation. When you unlock your true essence and reclaim the power already within you, you begin to lead from a place of purpose and passion.

Imagine a career where joy and happiness are not tied to endless to-do lists or financial milestones but rooted in a deeper sense of fulfillment. That fulfillment comes from being connected to your true human-*being*.

When you know who you are and what you uniquely bring, you are free to walk your own path and choose your steps forward with confidence.

You are powerful. You are capable. You are resilient. You have wisdom, skill, and drive. And if you want to rise to your full potential, it begins by claiming your true worth.

### An Introduction to the Four Principles

*SelfPowerment* is built on the understanding that true success is not just measured by what you achieve, but by how you live and experience your life, personally and professionally. It provides a structured yet flexible path that empowers high-achieving women to break free from external expectations and realign with their inner power—their *"I am … "*

At the heart of the framework are four interconnected core principles. Each one represents a key part of the transformational journey:

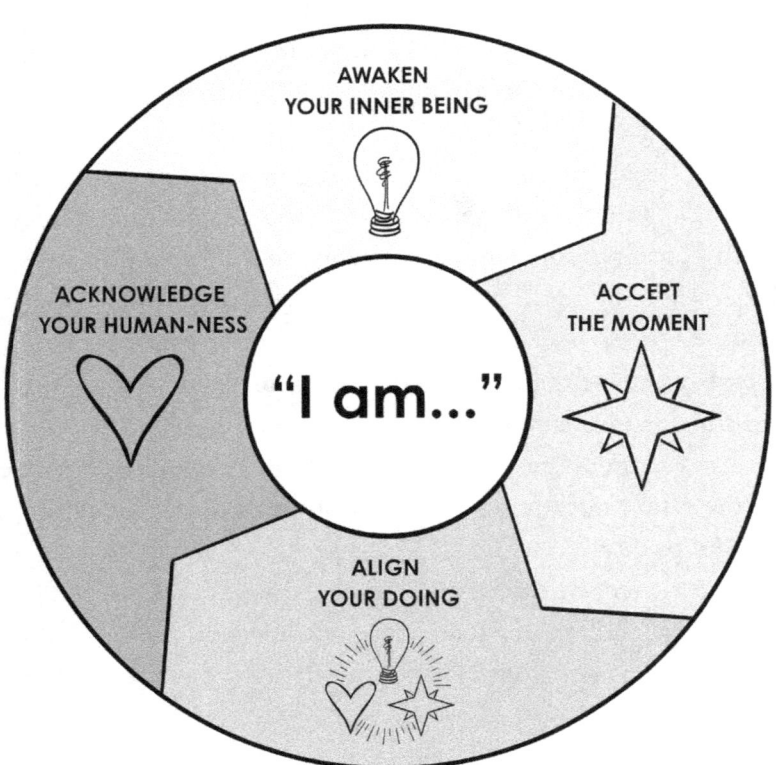

Each principle helps you explore a different aspect of your *"I am ...,"* guiding you through self-awareness, self-expression, and ultimately into your inner power.

Together, these principles form a powerful guide, helping you navigate toward a life and career that reflect your true self, your purpose, and your definition of fulfillment.

Though the *SelfPowerment* journey is designed to move through the principles in order, the framework is fluid. You can revisit it regularly as a tool to reset and realign.

Depending on what you're facing, whether it's a new opportunity, a professional challenge, a season of change, or your own personal journey of awareness, you may find yourself drawn more deeply into one principle than another.

## 1. Acknowledge Your Human-ness

This first principle is the foundation of self-discovery. It invites you to step away from the noise—beyond your roles, responsibilities, and daily demands—and simply connect with yourself as a human. It's an intentional pause to honor your physical body, your brilliant mind, and your full emotional life.

*Acknowledgement* of your human-ness brings you closer to understanding your unique strengths and natural capabilities, even disabilities. It also creates space to identify and begin to let go of limiting beliefs and generational patterns that may have been holding you back.

By embracing your full humanity, you gain a deeper and more honest awareness of your strengths and human powers. This opens the door to authentic self-worth and confidence rooted in your true *"I am ... "*

## 2. Awaken Your Inner Being

This principle centers on the *being* part of your human-*being*. It is the invitation to uncover your true purpose, feel your inner power, and listen to your inner voice stopping the full consumption of striving, forcing, or proving.

When you awaken to your inner being, you become aware, you become mindful of the stillness within, and you notice where peace, joy, and fulfillment naturally begin to rise.

*Awakening* involves gently peeling back the layers of emotions like fear, anxiety, regret, and sadness, along with the pressures and expectations from your life journey that may have become buried in your soul.

You start to learn how to quiet the noise in your head, manage the self-doubt, and find stillness. It begins with a pause. Then a breath. Then finding that stillness and feeling of *being* inside of you in the moment, not your *thoughts*.

This stillness isn't passive; it is a powerful space where self-doubt begins to fade, where self-love and sufficiency take root.

When you slow down and reconnect with your *"I am …,"* your wisdom and intuition begin to emerge, and you can hear it. In that quiet, you remember who the essence of your being is.

## 3. Accept the Moment

As you continue around the framework, this next principle leads you to fully embrace the present moment and to accept all of life's experiences—both the joyful and the difficult. This principle allows you to look up and see all the infinite possibilities available to you.

*Acceptance* does not mean resignation. Instead, it gives you the power to stop fighting what is outside your control and discover what's possible in the here and now.

This principle positions you to take full responsibility and accountability for your life and career. You aren't merely a passive participant in your story. Your human-*being* is always present and powerful, able to help you take ownership of your life.

When you accept the present moment without resistance, you create space to make courageous and intentional choices. You stop chasing outcomes, let life unfold in front of you, and step forward with peace and freedom.

Through *Acceptance*, you reclaim the power of choice and take action rooted in your *"I am ..."*

## 4. Align Your Doing

The final principle is about ensuring that *what* you do and *how* you do it reflect who you truly are. *Alignment* helps you connect your self-image, intentions, and outward actions with your inner truth and purpose.

Rather than letting your job title, calendar, or to-do list define you, this principle reminds you to bring your human-*being* into every moment of doing. With clarity and calm, you can move through your roles and responsibilities in a way that honors your true self.

In *Alignment*, you step into your true self, with your presence, your voice, and your energy. You are no longer reacting or on autopilot but becoming who you are with intent and purpose. This is where true manifestation happens. When you are aligned, you naturally build authentic connections, cultivate resilience, and lead with confidence and purpose.

\* \* \*

To help you fully apply these four core principles, the next section introduces eight key strategies—two for each principle. These strategies are practical, actionable, and grounded in real-life examples from women who have embraced *SelfPowerment* in their own journeys.

When you connect to your *"I am ..."* and begin to live from the inside out, you step away from chasing success for its own sake. You begin to live from purpose. You create space for joy.

Together, the four principles and eight strategies will guide your transformation—from a life shaped by outside achievements to one led by inner fulfillment.

Through *SelfPowerment*, you'll learn how to live in alignment with your authentic self. This is what it means to become a human-*being*, *doing*.

# The *SelfPowerment* Framework

Women are all unique and incredible. Among us, there is a wide and equally valuable range of leadership traits and styles.

Unlike empowerment, which suggests someone else grants you power, *SelfPowerment* is about recognizing that the power already resides within you.

At the heart of the *SelfPowerment* Framework is your *"I am ..."*, the ever-present core of your true self. It is the unchanging, authentic identity that lives beneath the layers of roles, labels, expectations, and experiences.

You are a human-*being* first, before all the doing.

While being rooted in your being is powerful, it also calls you to take true deep ownership of your doing. You are the only one who can live your life. You are responsible to walk your own path.

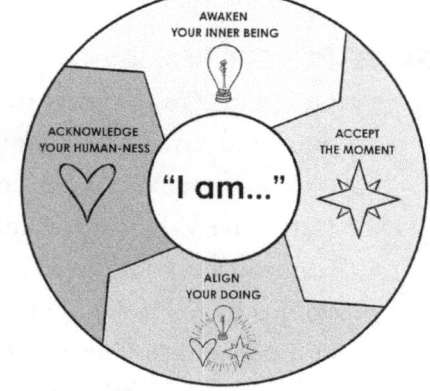

The four principles of *SelfPow-erment* offer steady checkpoints—reminding you to pause, assess, and realign, no matter the season or situation you're in. These four guiding principles are:

1. Acknowledge Your Human-ness
2. Awaken Your Inner Being
3. Accept the Moment
4. Align Your Doing

When these principles are paired with the eight practical strategies (presented in the chapters that follow), they shift the way you lead and live from being driven by external achievements to being grounded in inner fulfillment. Your *doing* becomes aligned with your human-*being*.

## ACTION

Declare that your *"I am ..."* is always enough. This simple truth can become the anchor for your next step forward.

## AFFIRMATIONS

*"I am enough."*
*"I am a human-being, doing."*
*"I am the only one who can live my life. No one else can do it for me."*

## PAUSE, REFLECT, REALIGN

- Go back to your answer to this question: If you opened your front door and saw an elephant standing there, what would you do? Now ask yourself: What does your response reveal about how you instinctively show up in unexpected moments of life or leadership?
- Can you feel your *"I am ...,"* your full human-being, separate from your doing? How might you bring more of your breath, energy, and essence into how you show up in this moment, just as you are?
- Of the four *SelfPowerment* principles, which one are you most drawn to in this season of your life? What does your pull toward this principle reveal about what you most need, desire, or are ready to shift within yourself?

# CHAPTER 10

# PRINCIPLE ONE: Acknowledge Your Human-ness

"Knowing yourself is the beginning
of all wisdom."

**~ Aristotle**

A lex stared at her monitor. Half a dozen tabs blinked back at her. Next to her computer, stacks of contracts and presentation notes were sprawled across the desk.

It was 9:43 p.m.

A Slack notification chimed, startling her. Apparently, she wasn't the only one online this late. Her inbox was still open, unread messages waiting. She clicked on one, skimmed the latest integration update, and sighed.

Since the last major reorganization, everyone at Trizenix was expected to keep pace with the new leadership's demands, but the pace felt endless.

She used to love this time of day. When the noise finally stopped, her thoughts could breathe. But lately, the quiet felt heavy.

Everyone had been stretched thin under the company's aggressive new growth strategy. The executive team had made it clear: there was no room for average performance this year.

Alex sat back in her chair and rubbed her temples. She had to push through; the current sales data had to be ready for tomorrow's leadership meeting.

James, the Vice President of Strategic Accounts, would be there. He was sharp, polished, and rising fast. He was also her main competitor for the newly announced Chief Sales Officer (CSO) role.

He wasn't a villain—far from it. He was a solid candidate. But after 15 years of grinding through the ranks, Alex had earned her title as Senior Vice President of Sales at Trizenix. Her drive and relentless commitment had made her the obvious choice.

She had been handpicked by the founder and board to help build what had become a respected technology firm. Her leadership had fueled client loyalty, driven repeat business, and resulted in year-over-year revenue growth.

But Trizenix had changed. With new capital investors came bigger goals, bolder forecasts, tighter timelines, and ambitious AI transformation plans. Everyone was being watched, measured, and compared.

And now the expectations felt heavier than ever. The CSO role would not only own revenue but also define the direction, culture, and future of the entire sales organization. It was the kind of responsibility Alex had spent her career preparing for.

Her Apple watch buzzed: "You can still do it. Take a walk today and get back on track."

Ugh. Why do I still have these notifications on?

Before things escalated at work, her morning walks were sacred—30 quiet minutes with her dog, a podcast, and the crisp morning air. By the time she returned, her thoughts were clear, her heart steady.

Now? She dragged herself from the office Keurig to her desk before sunrise for nonstop calls, updates, and executive reviews.

Sleep could wait.

Alex stood and stretched, her back aching from hours at her desk. She crossed the quiet room and looked out the window into the dark night, letting her eyes rest from the harsh glow of the screen.

That's when she saw her reflection in the window.

She had to admit, she looked exhausted. A woman with hunched shoulders, tired eyes, and a tight line for a mouth stared back. She barely recognized herself.

And in contrast, there on her desk sat a photo from the Big Sur team retreat two years ago.

Alex saw herself standing in the sun with her team, smiling widely. Her eyes sparkled. Renée, her mentor and long-time CEO of Trizenix, stood beside her. That night, they had toasted record-breaking results and her promotion to SVP.

She stared at that image for a long moment. *What happened to me?*

She closed her eyes and sighed. While she used to live and lead with passion, now she was just trying to keep her head above water.

Her calendar was crammed with strategy syncs, performance briefings, and executive visibility meetings. She had missed most of her son's baseball season and barely made it to her daughter's senior recital. She hadn't gone to Pilates in a month or met a friend for brunch. She felt like a machine.

Performing. Producing. Pushing.

Just a human-*doing*.

And with that grind came doubts.

What if the board really wanted someone younger? Someone like James, sharp, articulate, and connected to the new leadership consultants?

Her assistant had warned her about something she overheard yesterday. James was chatting in the break room with one of the operations guys, and had said, "Alex is great—but she's 'old Trizenix' through and through."

Her mind raced. What if I have peaked? What if they want something new, not something proven? What if I don't fit this next phase?

A weight settled on her chest.

Alex had survived burnout before like during the SaaS overhaul years ago, but this? This felt different.

She looked again at the photo. She remembered that feeling of being confident, energized, and clear. She knew who she was. She executed in the zone. She was ready for anything.

Right now? She felt like a shadow of her former self.

And then an unfamiliar thought crossed her mind: *Is this even worth it anymore?*

A quiet acknowledgment overcame her: she felt lost. She had been chasing results for so long, she'd forgotten how to simply be still with just herself.

In that moment, something shifted. Not really a breakthrough, but a recognition. A clear, quiet awareness: *I have become so busy doing and achieving that I have disconnected from who I really am.*

Something had to change.

* * *

## Honoring Who You Are

At one point or another in her career, almost every woman will hit a bump in the road. Perhaps you can relate. Maybe you've been downsized, or perhaps you were passed over for a promotion. It could be a colleague or supervisor who humiliated you in a meeting, or that time in a board meeting when you thought you were prepared, only to be caught off guard.

Whether it's dealing with unexpected events, surviving a personal or family crisis, or even getting the big opportunity and feeling in over your head, your confidence is shaken, and doubt sneaks in. In the midst of the clutter and noise, you lose sight of who you are.

We've all been there. That's why the first principle of *SelfPowerment* is *Acknowledge Your Human-ness.*

More than a surface-level check-in, this principle invites you to dive deep into your human-ness—to know, value, and love the essence of who you are.

Aristotle, one of the greatest philosophers and polymaths in history, has had a profound influence on Western thought and culture. He said something simple yet so insightful: "Knowing yourself is the beginning of all wisdom."

Those words underline the essential nature of self-awareness for the journey to self-worth and self-confidence. Wisdom and growth begin with an honest understanding of who you truly are.

By knowing yourself, you lay the groundwork for a life of purpose and achievement, where your unique gifts can truly shine.

By acknowledging your strengths and understanding what you excel at and love to do, you discover your unique superpowers.

Confidence and power are not bestowed upon you; they are cultivated through recognizing and leveraging your unique talents and gifts.

When you acknowledge and embrace all of your capabilities—your strengths and weaknesses—and let go of limiting beliefs, clarity rises to the surface.

*Acknowledgment* is about going back to the center, to your *"I am ... "* and honoring all that you are as a human.

## My Early Influences

Looking at my own human-ness has been a journey. While the elephant question marked a turning point in understanding myself, the roots of who I am go much deeper.

Raised by a trailblazing single mother, a first-generation American, I grew up immersed in values of resilience, independence, and hard work. My mom courageously broke many generational cycles from her Greek culture and family traditions. After my parents' divorce when I was four (in 1959 divorce was rare, especially in the Greek family structure), my mother made it her mission for my sister and me to break more generational cycles, such as achieving financial independence.

She encouraged us toward careers in the emerging computer industry and taught us to never depend on anyone else—especially a man—for money, to strive for self-sufficiency, and to stay true to ourselves, always. Her strong, brave, independent voice echoed as the foundation of my life and career.

Throughout my school years, I naturally gravitated toward leadership roles. I became the first female class president of both my junior and senior high school classes, led fundraisers, and was often named "hardest worker" in the yearbook.

At the same time, I silently battled undiagnosed dyslexia and ADHD (attention-deficit/hyperactivity disorder). I found ways to adapt and excel in math and hands-on sciences, thriving in advanced classes, effectively learning and growing—yet never fully reading a book, never reading aloud, or writing stellar papers. Yet I leaned into what worked with my superpowers, instinctively.

And by playing to my strengths, I succeeded in college-prep and honors classes.

My natural tendencies fueled my drive and determination, which were further shaped and reinforced by my parents and the experiences of my childhood.

Those same tendencies also served me well in my first job and would eventually propel me into a fast-rising corporate career. Starting as a COBOL programmer at Liberty Mutual, I quickly earned promotion after promotion in the fast-growing world of insurance technology, where I led teams and delivered major IT development projects.

For me, success meant financial reward and independence. I exceeded expectations, pushed hard, constantly got tapped for the latest big strategic project, and always aimed for the next promotion.

My answer to the elephant question captured that mindset: "Ride it, then sell it!"

But eventually, roadblocks came.

I started to feel the weight of the glass ceiling. Despite my results, achievements, and qualifications, I was told I "wasn't strategic"—a critique I later learned was common for women leaders. And for the first time ever, I genuinely feared getting a "meets expectations" performance review, all because of "style."

The pressure triggered anxiety, fear, and ultimately, panic attacks. So, I sought professional cognitive therapy.

I began to learn how I was wired.

That's when small things began to become clear and shift. My therapist diagnosed my learning differences but highlighted how they actually didn't hold me back. For the first time, I began to truly acknowledge my full self—strengths and limitations included.

Through therapy, I came to see the importance of breaking free from my own personal set of generational cycles that were holding me back. While my mother's teachings had fueled my drive, I started to get a glimpse that true success isn't just about achievement for others.

Therapy gave me tools and actual names for my patterns, helping to crack open the door and gain clarity.

I started to look up and out and ask myself: *Why not me? Why not become a consultant?*

\* \* \*

After 19 years at Liberty Mutual, a company I had believed would be my place until retirement, I made a bold move. I left.

I stepped into the unknown, choosing growth over comfort. This was not just a change of job; it was a pivotal step in my journey toward greater self-awareness.

That decision took me to KPMG, opening a new path. It was there that I learned all the aspects of consulting. It set the trajectory that would eventually lead me to become a strategic advisor and researcher.

Still, when the season at KPMG ended abruptly, I was rattled.

Working with executive coaches, I started to identify some of my superpowers beyond just execution. I returned to my human center once again and began to ask deeper questions: *What type of culture would help me thrive? What type of role and company do I align with? What truly lights me up?*

I also began to consider the type of company I wanted to work for next, the culture I needed to thrive in, and what truly fueled my passion. What emerged was a new vision of *Why not me?*

I set my sights on becoming a Gartner-like analyst and industry thought leader. That dream led me to TowerGroup, where I became Vice President U.S. Insurance Practice Lead. I developed from being a consultant into becoming an analyst, researcher, speaker, and trusted voice across the industry.

This phase was about more than professional success. I also began investing in myself physically, mentally, and emotionally. Self-care became part of my rhythm rather than a luxury. It helped me manage anxiety and reconnect with my human-ness.

Executive coaching revealed more: I wasn't just a doer and taskmaster. I was a strategist, a visionary, and a wise woman. That clarity and confidence in my expanded capabilities empowered me to launch my own business.

An investor once told me, "Jump and a net will appear." So, I jumped.

I launched Strategy Meets Action and in doing so, I broke the generational cycle of requiring financial security, something that was part of my heritage.

For 15 years, I successfully led SMA through a recession, a pandemic, and eventually a successful acquisition. But that growth was only possible because I was deeply grounded in my whole self—my human-ness.

Each step, each lesson, connected. I grew from executor to female executive leader, from achiever to visionary.

Throughout my career, I embraced the full range of who I was, earning titles like chief information officer, chief transformation officer, partner, vice president, founder, and chief executive officer. I realized that they were just roles, not my identity.

Even now, I continue to learn about myself, grow, and evolve. The dyslexic girl who struggled with reading and writing is now building the *SelfPowerment* platform.

\* \* \*

When we fully acknowledge our human-ness—when we know, accept, and love who we are—we gain clarity and confidence. We let go of limitations, of what other people think about us, and what we should be. We live aligned with our gifts. We lead with ease.

When we invest time in *Acknowledgment*, the return is confidence and self-worth.

From there, the possibilities are limitless.

## LIVING IT OUT

The four principles are your guide. But to move with power and alignment, you need strategy.

## STRATEGIES IN THIS PRINCIPLE

1. **Harness Your Powers**: More than listing your strengths, this is about owning them and stepping boldly into what makes you brilliant.
2. **Invest in Self-Care**: This isn't just pampering. This is about believing you're worth the investment—body, mind, and soul. The return is exponential.

In the next chapters, we'll explore these strategies with practical tools and stories from women who are living them out.

And with each principle, you'll find an affirmation to help you access and uplift your inherent goodness and worth within. Remember: the way you speak to yourself shapes how you live. The first action you can take to choose your own power is to speak words of clarity and strength over yourself.

I encourage you to start by speaking these words of affirmation to yourself.

## AFFIRMATION

*"I know, love, and accept my human-ness."*

Embrace who you are—strengths, weaknesses, and everything in between. Let go of limiting beliefs, generational cycles, and self-doubts, and step into the power that was always yours.

## CHAPTER 11

# Strategy 1: Harness Your Powers

Every woman I've worked with, mentored, coached, or interviewed has achieved success on paper. Many hold senior titles and lead impressive teams.

Yet when I ask, "Do you feel confident and ready for any career opportunity?" most hesitate.

Some whisper, "Not really."

In those quiet, honest moments, I hear how just one event, one person, or one comment can rattle even the strongest and most successful woman. Suddenly, confidence crumbles and doubt takes the lead.

Why does this happen to so many of us? And more importantly, how do we reclaim the power we already have?

### Confidence Types

Through my research and interviews, I uncovered three types of confidence among successful women. It's important to remember that confidence type does not determine career growth or achievement—all of these women are highly accomplished. However, there was one type that navigated challenges with strength and ease.

- **Steadfast Until Shaken**: Women with this type of confidence are grounded but easily rocked by setbacks like a layoff, a toxic boss, or even a planned career pause, like maternity leave. When the unexpected happens, self-doubt rushes in.
- **Underlying Imposter Syndrome**: Women with this type of confidence appear confident on the surface, but inside they're striving, second-guessing, and waiting for the next validation. When expectations are unclear, they lose momentum and question their value.
- **Centered and Confident**: Women with this type of confidence lead from a foundation of deep self-awareness. They trust their gifts and respond to adversity with resilience and intention.

The first two types often appeared confident and competent on the outside, but inside they struggled with feeling like they weren't enough. And at some point, the fear of failure or other limiting beliefs held them down or held them back.

The third type, on the other hand, carried themselves through ups and downs without wavering. What separates this group from the others isn't a title or training. It's that they've done the inner work. They know who they are and what they bring.

## Fighting a Culture of Doubt

If your confidence has waned at times, take heart. You are not alone. Corporate culture hasn't always welcomed women's voices. According to the 2024 McKinsey study, *Women in the Workplace*:[7]

- 40% of women say their judgment is questioned in areas where they're the expert
- 40% are interrupted or spoken over more than others (men)
- 20% are mistaken for someone at a much lower level

As women, we're often working twice as hard to be seen, heard, and valued—and that daily grind can erode even the most hard-earned confidence.

The antidote is to become a *SelfPowered* woman. But *SelfPowerment* doesn't come from titles or approval. It's a choice. A practice. You decide what voice to listen to. You choose to lead from your core.

## What's Your "Elephant Moment"?

A powerful moment in my research came from a single question: If you opened your front door and saw an elephant, what would you do?

The women I interviewed gave wildly different answers. Each one revealed a natural leadership trait.

| Response | Leadership Style |
|---|---|
| Shut the door | Protective, risk-averse |
| Touch it | Reflective, observant |
| Call a zookeeper | Pragmatic, a problem solver |
| Take a picture | Engaged, an influencer |
| Triage it | Empathetic, a caregiver |
| Feed it | Generous, a nurturer |
| Use it | Resourceful, practical |
| Ride it | Adventurous, bold |
| Sell it | Entrepreneurial, opportunistic |
| Name it | Personal, a connector |
| Ask why it's here | Philosophical, a visionary |

There's no wrong answer! What matters is recognizing your instinct and owning your style. *Harnessing* your power starts by recognizing it.

## Your Superpowers Are Already at Work

Your strengths often feel invisible to you because they come naturally. But that's exactly why they matter. When something feels effortless, it's often a gift in disguise.

> **RESEARCH SPOTLIGHT**
>
> "I didn't go to college,
> but I built a $2-billion practice.
> I know the business.
> I know what *good* looks like.
> I can see when we're slipping—
> and I speak up.
> My superpowers are
> translating complexity into clarity,
> building trust,
> and delivering impact.
> I don't wait for permission—
> I saddle up and ride that elephant."
>
> ~ **Laura | Senior Managing Director**

Think back through your career. What are you proud of? What came easily? What do others consistently ask you for?

You'll start to spot the patterns. Maybe it's your ability to inspire. Maybe it's simplifying complexity. Maybe it's seeing trends others miss.

Indra Nooyi, former CEO of PepsiCo, calls it your "hip-pocket skill." The one thing people always count on you for.

For her, it was breaking down complexity. For me, it used to be executing and delivering results.

Now, it's seeing infinite possibilities from emerging patterns and trends.

If you're unsure of your superpowers, don't worry. I didn't clearly name mine until my 60s. But they were always there, guiding me and shaping how I worked and led.

## Esther's Story: Think Forward, Lead Boldly

Esther's career journey is a masterclass in the power of self-awareness and confident execution. With roles such as president of a global tech company and CIO of a major bank, her résumé speaks volumes. But it's her mindset that truly defines her.

Esther has always known her strengths: strategic thinking, people alignment, and the ability to quickly assess complex business challenges.

"Think forward," she often says. It's a mantra that has guided her into high-impact roles others might have hesitated to take.

When passed over for a promotion, Esther didn't shrink. She sought a mentor, recalibrated, and positioned herself for even greater opportunity.

When told she might not go far in sales, she got a call from a former leader and took a leap into a job she wasn't "qualified for" on paper. But her hip-pocket skills carried her through.

"I've had various roles in my career, and with each, I applied a consistent methodology of forward thinking: getting in and understanding a business, understanding what the issues were both top-down and bottom-up," said Esther. "It's about taking a strategic view, understanding the landscape, and then diving deep into the details. By leveraging this approach, I've been able to lead effectively, regardless of the industry or challenge."

While many women wrestle with imposter syndrome, Esther never did. She acknowledged her human-ness but never doubted her capability. That clarity, that self-trust, is what attracted leaders to tap her again and again.

Esther's story is a call to all women: Know your powers. Own your strengths. And when opportunity calls, say yes! You already have what it takes.

## Leading From the Inside Out

Once you name your powers, everything changes. You speak with conviction. You make decisions from clarity. You show up with presence.

To be *SelfPowered*, you must own your strengths, honor them, and *Harness* them.

## CHAPTER 12

# Strategy 2: Invest in Self-Care

*SelfPowerment* begins by honoring our human-ness, and that includes acknowledging our limits.

For years, I believed I could power through anything. Like so many women I've coached and interviewed, I equated strength with stamina. I told myself I'd rest later, after the next deliverable, the next event, the next milestone.

But "later" kept moving. Eventually, I hit a wall.

Sound familiar?

It wasn't until my health took a hit—when I had what I thought was a heart attack but turned out to be a panic attack—that I realized something had to change. I had to stop treating myself like a machine. I needed to honor my limits, listen to my body, and tend to my mind and spirit. I needed self-care.

Self-care is more than finally stopping for a spa day or scheduling a long-overdue brunch with a friend, then patting ourselves on the back for doing it. It's more than taking that annual vacation and checking it off the list. When we do that, we refill just enough to keep going, at least until the check-engine light comes on again.

*Investing* in self-care is a foundational strategy to go from survival to *thriving*. It's about maintaining the capacity to lead, live, and love without losing yourself in the process.

In my research, only 25% of women reported consistently prioritizing self-care. Not surprisingly, these women showed greater resilience, clearer decision-making, and deeper personal fulfillment than the other 75%.

Self-care is more than a moment. It's a mindset. A rhythm. A commitment to stay whole as you rise.

## Fuel and Fire

As women, we are natural caregivers and high achievers. Like the matriarch elephants who lead their herd with intuition and strength, we manage, respond, guide, and protect. We pour ourselves out for work, for our families, and for our communities.

But pouring out without pouring back in leaves us empty.

I spent years pushing myself to the edge. When I had a major panic attack, it became a wake-up call. As I learned to acknowledge my humanness and be accountable to myself, I realized I had been ignoring my needs. So, I reintroduced self-care into my routine. The stressors and responsibilities didn't go away. But I began to ride the wave instead of being drowned by it.

Self-care became my foundation—not a luxury or emergency response, but a non-negotiable necessity.

Tech executive, philanthropist, and author Sheryl Sandberg often emphasizes that true resilience is built on self-care, saying, "You can't lead others or achieve your goals if you're running on empty."[8]

When you invest in yourself—consistently and intentionally—you build the strength to lead with clarity and calm.

## The Mind–Body Connection

Your body is wise. It sends signals when it needs attention: fatigue, tension, restlessness.

Yet only one in four women in our study maintained consistent physical practices. Those who did—whether by walking, running, hiking, dancing, swimming, gardening, or engaging in strength training or yoga—not only felt stronger but also reported having better mental clarity and emotional regulation.

> **RESEARCH SPOTLIGHT**
> "Regular exercise
> and sufficient sleep
> are essential for maintaining
> my mental clarity
> and overall well-being,
> enabling me to perform at my best
> professionally and personally."
>
> **~ Leigh | Chief Executive Officer**

### Intellectual and Emotional Fuel

But self-care also includes how we feed our minds.

In early career stages, this might look like certifications or coursework. Later, it may become mentorship, coaching, reading, and learning from peers. But all too often, these get deprioritized.

Your growth matters. Feeding your mind is an act of power.

The same is true for your heart and spirit. Soul care—whether through prayer, journaling, chanting, meditation, or spending time in nature—showed up in subtle but consistent ways among the most grounded leaders in our study.

Business may be built on action, but transformation is fueled by investing in your body, mind, and soul.

### Research Reflections

Here's what we learned from the interviews...

| Category | Common Practices | Research Findings |
|---|---|---|
| Body | Walking or running, hiking in nature, swimming, dancing, doing ballet, going to the gym, doing strength training or personal training, doing yoga and Pilates, prioritizing sleep | • Many women lacked consistency<br>• Physical care often only began after burnout or health concerns<br>• Support systems made a significant difference<br>• Older and younger women alike cited a lack of time as their biggest barrier |
| Mind | Reading (fiction and nonfiction), listening to podcasts, attending workshops and conferences for professional development and ongoing learning, going to therapy, having a coach or a mentor, doing daily mind puzzles | • Early career learning was high but tapered off<br>• Few had formal executive coaches; peer mentoring was more common<br>• Coping strategies ranged from healthy ones to simply numbing |
| Soul | Having spiritual practices or rituals including prayer, meditation, and mindfulness, doing breathwork, going on nature walks, gardening, participating in spiritual retreats | • Many didn't label these as "soul care," yet agreed that these fostered peace and were grounding<br>• Practices varied widely, from structured religion to deeply personal spiritual routines, including spending time in nature |

## Jessica's Story: Running Toward Clarity

For Jessica, a CEO leading a billion-dollar enterprise, running isn't about fitness; it's her sanctuary. Whether she's untangling a business problem, shedding stress from a high-stakes meeting, or simply reclaiming a moment of stillness, her feet hitting the pavement is a grounding practice for her.

"Running has always been a thing that helps me get it out of my system—whatever *it* is," shared Jessica. "It gives me time to think, solve problems, or just get the stress out. The introvert in me needs some time to recharge."

Beyond stress relief, this regular act of self-care also offers space for movement and breathing that allows her best insights to rise. In fact, one of the most significant ideas of her career, the model that earned her a patent, was born mid-run. She still remembers the exact road where it came to her.

In the quiet rhythm of her stride, Jessica returns to herself—not CEO, not strategist, just who she is.

> **RESEARCH SPOTLIGHT**
> "I'm big on carving out time for things I like, such as yoga. I make time to do that, and I get the support from my family because they know it is a stress reliever."
>
> ~ **Rachel | Chief Executive Officer**

## The Myth of Balance

You are not here to achieve perfect balance. *That* doesn't exist.

The most grounded women in our research weren't juggling perfectly—they were making intentional choices. They prioritized what mattered most in that season. And they let go of guilt.

According to a 2024 report by the Gender Equality Policy Institute, women still spend twice as much time on household tasks as men, regardless of age.[9] And among full-time workers who are also caring for children, aging parents, or both, 56% are women.[10]

While we may not be able to change that reality, we can choose to protect our energy.

Self-care isn't selfish; it's strategic. It's not a reward for reaching the end of your list; it's a way of living, leading, and showing up whole.

You matter. Your needs matter. And the world needs what only you can give—strong, whole, and deeply cared for.

To be *SelfPowered*, you must first be self-fueled.

# PRINCIPLE ONE: Acknowledge Your Human-ness

Something powerful happens when a woman stops proving and starts pausing—when she takes a moment to truly see herself not for what she does, but for who she is.

Throughout this principle, we explored what it means to return to your center, to acknowledge all of you: your gifts, your wiring, your story, your needs.

The first strategy, *Harness Your Powers*, invited you to look beneath the surface and name the strengths that have been quietly guiding you all along. Maybe they're the traits others always count on you for. Maybe they show up in your elephant answer. Either way, they are yours to own.

Then we turned to *Invest in Self-Care*—not as a treat or reward, but as a leadership practice. You began to ask: *What fuels me? Where am I depleted? And what do I need—not just to keep going, but to grow?* Whether it's moving your body, feeding your mind, or tending to your spirit, self-care is how we stay rooted in our power.

Together, these two strategies offer something deeper than productivity or performance. They offer grounding. They remind you that your worth isn't measured by what you deliver, but by the truth of your *"I am ..."*

When you name your strengths and honor your needs, you begin to lead—not from exhaustion or ego, but from wholeness.

## ACTION
Take a quiet moment this week to write down two things:
- A strength that comes naturally to you—something others often appreciate or rely on you for.
- One small way you can care for yourself this week—something simple that brings you peace, energy, or joy.

Let these two truths guide how you move through the week, with clarity and compassion.

## STRATEGIES IN THIS PRINCIPLE
1. Harness Your Powers
2. Invest in Self-Care

## AFFIRMATIONS
*"I am powerful because I know who I am."*
*"I am worthy of care, attention, and compassion."*
*"I know, love, and accept my human-ness."*

## PAUSE, REFLECT, REALIGN
- What part of your human-ness—a strength, passion, or leadership style—have you been hesitant to embrace or forgotten entirely? Are you ready to harness it more fully? As you embrace your capability, can you feel an inner shift happening?
- What limiting beliefs about yourself do you most often return to when you're stressed or uncertain? Where did those come from, and are they still true? How might those be holding you back or creating self-doubt?

- What does your body, mind, or soul need that you've been ignoring? What would it look like to respond to those needs with care?
- What's one "flaw" or perceived weakness that might actually be a hidden strength or part of your superpower? How could embracing it bring about an inner shift on your perspective?

## CHAPTER 13

# PRINCIPLE TWO: Awaken Your Inner Being

"Being must be felt. It can't be thought."

**~ Eckhart Tolle**

A lex pulled her Audi into the underground garage beneath the Trizenix headquarters downtown. Thanks to construction traffic, she only had 15 minutes before the executive sales meeting on the 23rd floor.

She pulled into her designated parking space a little too fast. Her heart pounded. Even though this was a standard weekly meeting, it was the first time the whole executive team would be in the same room since the CSO succession process had been announced. The conversation upstairs would be high stakes. She had to pull herself together.

A rush of heat climbed up her neck onto her cheeks; even her ears burned. She unclipped her seatbelt, but her lungs still felt tight, and her heart raced. *Not now*, the thought flashed through her mind.

Her fingers gripped the steering wheel like a lifeline. *Was it always this stuffy down here?*

Just breathe, she coaxed herself. Inhale 1-2-3-4 …, Alex counted. Hold for 4. Then exhale … 5-6-7-8.

Finally, she felt her heartbeat begin to slow. One more time—breathe in … hold it … feel the air flow through your lips.

As the wave of panic passed, Alex leaned against the steering wheel and closed her eyes. *You don't have time for this.*

Between high-profile client reviews, performance pressure, and managing a sales team hungry for direction, she barely had time to think, let alone have a meltdown.

*Get a grip, Alexandra,* she told herself. She reached into her bag for her lipstick—one last layer of armor before walking into a room of sharp minds and sharper agendas.

Upstairs, the talk would center on sales forecasts, cultural alignment, and leadership presence. James, the Vice President of Strategic Accounts, would be there, as always collected, confident, and fully prepared. She liked him. They'd both been working toward this for years. And now they were both being watched.

Alex used to feel unshakable in those meetings. She could shift a room with her voice, her vision. But lately … something felt off.

She checked her reflection in the visor mirror. "You've got this," she whispered. Then, shoulders squared, she stepped out of the car and quickly walked toward the elevators.

The meeting went well, and Alex was relieved.

Later that night, Alex sat on the edge of her bed, laptop still open beside her, glancing over at the never-ending Slack and email messages. The latest message from one of her regional leads blinked at the corner of the screen—another urgent request, another urgent update.

This time, she didn't answer.

She closed her laptop and set it aside, then reached for the brown leather journal on her nightstand, the one she hadn't touched in months.

She leaned back against the pillows and flipped through the pages, stopping at an entry from last year.

In the middle of the page, she had written a quote: *"When things get loud, don't forget your why."*

She stared at the quote. What was her *why* now?

For years, it had been about building possibility: for her team, her clients, and herself. She loved the challenge and creativity of growth as well as the sales process itself. She loved helping clients imagine what was possible. Developing people into confident, purpose-driven leaders. Turning business goals into meaningful outcomes.

But lately, despite being in the running for the top sales role, it all felt strangely hollow—like she was running in circles. The meetings, the metrics, the polished executive presence—it looked like progress, but she wondered at times if she was losing touch with what mattered.

Worse, she was starting to believe the voices in her head:

*Maybe I'm not the best person for the job.*

*Maybe James fits the future better than I do.*

*Maybe I've outgrown this … or it's outgrown me.*

Her inner dialogue was relentless—a steady hum of thoughts and questions.

She turned to a blank page, picked up her pen, and began to write:

*Am I not good enough?*

*Am I relevant?*

*Have I lost my edge?*

She underlined *enough*, *relevant*, and *edge*. Three times. Then her hand slowed, and a new sentence emerged.

I don't know if I want this anymore.

She stared at the words. They were uncomfortable and comforting at the same time.

Alex set her pen down, reached over, and turned off the light. She sat in the darkness for a while, just thinking.

She didn't have the answers yet, but something had cracked open.

\* \* \*

## Reconnecting with Your Inner Being

You didn't get to this point in your career by strolling through the garden, and neither did I.

We are achievers. Executors. We know how to move fast, solve problems, and get things done in a world that rewards constant motion. But if we want to connect with the power of our inner being, we must pause—even briefly—and release our grip on the striving and doing.

While the first principle, *Acknowledge Your Human-ness*, may have affirmed truths you already recognized, this next principle might stretch you.

*Awakening* their inner being is unfamiliar to many. For others, it's challenging to fully embrace this idea within the context of a high-pressure, fast-paced business world. We are trained to think, analyze, and drive forward.

Yet, as Eckhart Tolle reminds us, if we want to connect with our inner being, we must step away from thinking. We must rediscover who we are beneath our thinking and doing.

This kind of stillness doesn't come naturally to most of us. Oprah Winfrey put it this way: "I had to learn to quiet the noise in my head, to realize that who I am is not the voice in my head, but the one who is aware of that voice."[11]

In my own journey, it took months of work with an executive coach for this truth to fully sink in. But once it did, the transformation was profound. My "aha!" moments became a turning point; embracing them changed my life.

Through this principle and its two strategies, you'll begin to cultivate stillness and anchor yourself in the strength of your human-ness and the power of your being. You'll begin to live from a place of inner alignment—where self-trust and self-love rise naturally, where you can hear and follow the quiet wisdom of your intuition.

Once you begin to recognize your being and connect it back to your human-ness, everything begins to come into focus.

### Stillness and Wonder

Have you ever noticed how nature always returns to balance?

I once watched a documentary on the animals of the savannah. The patience of the videographer amazed me—waiting for hours in total stillness to capture a single moment of action. But what impressed me most was the instinctive rhythm of the animals themselves.

Gazelles graze peacefully in the tall grass. Then one becomes aware—ears perk, head lifts. A pair of lionesses crouches in the distance. In an instant, the stillness turns into a blur of motion. The herd scatters. The chase begins. The lions close in on the slowest and weakest.

And then … quiet.

Moments later, the gazelles are back to grazing.

Stillness returns. Nature always finds its way back.

But we humans are different. Our minds keep spinning. Our storms never seem to end.

In our human-ness, we carry thoughts, emotions, fears, and responsibilities, all wrapped in a constant hum of external demands. Unless we intentionally stop and choose stillness, we live in a steady state of tension, constantly toggling between planning, proving, and performing.

Besides the flurry of external noise, you have been trained to intellectualize everything. From your education to your work, you learned to operate by thinking: to spot, identify, and assess.

You look outside the window and notice something tall and green. *Look at the broad leaves and little acorns. That must be an oak tree.* Your eyes scan up the trunk and over the beautiful branches. *Hmm, it's probably about 25 feet high*, you think as you notice how it compares to the height of your window.

You and I have been taught to evaluate everything.

That's our human-ness.

But the *being* looks out at the tree in awe and wonder. And in that moment, there is quiet and stillness.

You are simply aware. And it is enough.

When we are born, we naturally live from our *being*. We rest in the arms of our caregivers and experience the world with fresh and pure delight in discovery. Our pure expression reflects our inner being. (If you've ever watched an infant discover their hands or feet for the first time, you've witnessed this.)

But things change quickly.

Everything you learn begins to be conditional.

Our parents begin to add layers based on their beliefs and cultural traditions. We go to school where we're judged and graded. We're right or we're wrong. We begin to live trying to stay within the parameters, right? We're told to organize and plan, to analyze and strategize, and to execute and deliver.

One by one, the pureness of our being becomes covered in layers of thinking and striving to meet expectations. External cultural norms layer on top of each other, covering our being. As a result, we forget or lose our essence.

*Awakening* is about lifting up all those layers to uncover our *being* within.

## Finding Me Beneath the Chaos

My own awakening didn't come easily.

Learning to peel away the layers and embrace stillness, I discovered the radiant energy of my spirit and consciousness. *Awakening* has been a profound journey, allowing the internal pulse of energy and heart to light my way, and with it, to discover my intuition, wisdom, and power.

This has enabled me to transcend circumstances and step forward with renewed purpose, joy, and peace. But it took a breakpoint for me to begin paying attention.

For years, I lived in overdrive. I commuted 150 miles a day through Boston traffic, juggling roles, chasing results, proving my worth.

The outside noise was relentless. But the inside was worse. Stress, striving, and self-pressure got wrapped around every goal.

In the quiet of the night, anxiety often found me. Full, deep sleep wouldn't come. My mind raced through endless to-do lists and imagined worst-case scenarios. Often, in the middle of the night, I'd jump out of bed in a state of pure panic, saying, "What am I going to do? What am I going to do? What am I going to do?"

I would try to shake it off as if it were nothing, splash water on my face, try to settle my racing heart, and attempt to get back to sleep.

Exhausted and still wired in the morning, I longed for rest that never quite arrived. What I didn't realize was that these were mini panic attacks, not bad dreams. I thought I was managing the stress. I told myself I would be fine. But like tremors before a big earthquake, I should have seen the signs.

I was sitting in Boston Garden, watching the Celtics, my favorite basketball team, take the lead. Then it hit. A strange sensation crept into my body, subtle at first. My chest grew tight, as if the air I was breathing had thickened.

My heart began to pound—not just quickly, but furiously, like it was trying to escape my chest.

The roar of the crowd faded to a distant hum. My breath caught. My hands tingled. Dizziness swirled around me like a warning I couldn't make sense of.

I turned to my husband and whispered, "I think I'm having a heart attack."

In that moment, fear didn't just creep in—it crashed through. I didn't understand what was happening, only that something deep inside me had gone off track. It felt like my body had been hijacked, like a wire had snapped somewhere within.

Waves of panic surged through me, crashing like breakers against the shore, then pulling everything in their path out to sea. Over and over again, they came.

I was certain my heart was failing me. Not metaphorically—*physically*.

And I wasn't sure I would make it through the night.

We rushed out of the arena and headed straight to the emergency room. After cardiac triage and multiple tests, the diagnosis came back: acute anxiety.

For years afterward, I went to therapy. Took medication. Tried to push forward.

I was told that anxiety was a condition that I would always have, like diabetes or high blood pressure, and I would always need to take medication.

No matter what I did, the pressure never let up. The glass ceiling pressed down harder. Still, I kept striving—because I didn't yet know another way to be. But the truth was, I was exhausted. Overweight. Unhealthy. And deeply unfulfilled.

Then, in 2005, something unexpected happened.

When I accepted the role at TowerGroup, something in me exhaled. The position aligned with my strengths and passions, and I stepped in with quiet hope that this chapter might feel different.

Then came a wave of change I never saw coming. The company was acquired by Mastercard, and with it came a new CEO—a woman. She didn't just shift our org chart; she reshaped the culture.

First, she dismantled the invisible good old boys' club, introducing transparency, accountability, and a growth strategy that gave space for voices like mine to lead.

Second, she tackled compensation equity head-on. She reviewed roles, titles, and pay across the company, and adjusted mine to match my male peers. For the first time in my career, I felt both seen and valued.

But it was her third decision that transformed me most. She brought in an executive coach for the senior leadership team, who was the perfect blend of wisdom, academic, and business savvy. She was also a blend of Western and Eastern culture, knowledge, and tools. She was an unconventional mix and a powerful one.

> "Between stimulus and response, there is a space. In that space is our power to choose our response. In our response lies our growth and our freedom."
>
> ~ **Viktor Frankl**[33]

Working with her, something began to shift. Not overnight. Not in one dramatic moment. But gradually, quietly—layer by layer.

She helped me see how the noise in my head was dragging me backward into the past with regret and forward into the future with fear.

Rarely, if ever, was I fully in the present. I was surviving. But I wasn't living.

She introduced me to the idea that between me and the world around me, there was space. And in that space, I had power. Not *control* over others or over circumstances. But power over how I showed up.

Power over my breath.

Over my thoughts.

Over my being.

And that changed everything.

Around that same time, something else unexpected entered my life—another thread in this *Awakening* I didn't yet know I was in.

While driving one morning, I tuned into a new format I'd never heard of before: the earliest versions of a podcast. It was Oprah. She was interviewing Eckhart Tolle on a *Super Soul Sunday* series, guiding listeners through Tolle's book *A New Earth,* chapter by chapter.

I didn't know then how pivotal that podcast series would become, but as I listened, something in me shifted. Recognized. Created the awareness of my being.

They spoke about the noise in the mind. The constant chatter that pulls us out of presence. The ego's voice, the pain bodies. Always comparing, always fearing, always needing to prove.

They spoke of stillness—not as passivity, but as power.

Of presence—not as luxury, but as liberation.

Of being—not as weakness, but as the truest kind of strength.

Every day during my commute, I'd listen. And slowly, I began to see what had been hidden under all my striving:

The wisdom within me.

The stillness I'd been craving.

The space between the thoughts.

Sometimes the noise in my head would come in like a storm—racing thoughts, looping doubts, spinning "what ifs."

Other times, the storm would start in my body—an ache, a tightening, a fatigue I'd grown too used to ignoring. I began to learn to accept things beyond my control.

But now, for the first time, I had language for it.

And better yet, I had tools.

My coach deepened the experience. She took me on walks through nature. We stood before a rock structure that had been shaped by millions of years of wind and time. She asked me to notice the dew clinging to a single leaf. To feel its resilience.

It wasn't striving. It wasn't proving.

It simply *was*.

That image stayed with me.

Around the same time, I started to incorporate breathwork into my day. Just three intentional breaths—before a meeting, while waiting in the elevator, or even sitting in traffic. And in those quiet seconds, I began to feel myself again.

Not the achiever. Not the partner. Not the woman trying to prove she belonged in the room. But the little girl I used to be—the one who played outside and felt joy just for being alive.

*Awakening* didn't happen in one moment. It came through many small moments of choosing stillness over chaos.

Of presence over panic.

Of being over doing.

As I practiced, something beautiful began to unfold...

I started trusting myself again.

In fact, *Awakening* and finding my inner stillness eventually allowed me to come off my daily anxiety medicines.

I let go of the old belief that self-doubt meant I wasn't strong.

I realized it could actually be an invitation.

Not to spiral—but to pause. To listen. To reconnect.

And with that, the wise woman within me finally had room to speak.

## The Space Between the Beats

Recognizing your inner being begins with stillness.

I don't know what you're carrying today—but I know it's a lot. Maybe it's a looming deadline, a challenging conversation, a sink full of dishes, or another hard headline in the news. The world rarely stops moving, and neither do we.

Yes, you are strong. You are capable. You know how to juggle, respond, and lead.

But for the next few moments, I invite you to pause. To breathe. To listen for the quiet beneath the noise.

Place your hand on your heart.

Feel it beating beneath your palm—the steady ba-boom ... ba-boom ... ba-boom of your life force.

Now, listen for the pause between the beats.

Take a slow, deep breath in ...

And now exhale—completely, intentionally.

Feel the emptiness at the end of your breath.

Let your awareness scan through your body.

Notice any sensation—the buzzing in your fingers, the tension in your shoulders, the aliveness in your legs or feet.

Feel the energy. Notice the stillness within.

This stillness, this breath, this space between the beats of your heart is the essence of your *being*.

"You are not the thinker," says Eckhart Tolle. "You are the awareness behind the thought."[12]

The core of your *"I am ... "* begins here—in this pause, in this presence.

When you return to this stillness, something shifts. The noise begins to fade. The tension begins to soften. Self-doubt loosens its grip, and your wise inner voice begins to rise.

From this space, your strength, your power, your purpose begin to emerge—not from what you do, but from who you are.

## LIVING IT OUT

*Awakening* is not a surface shift—it's a pivotal step in living *SelfPowered*. It bridges your human-ness with your inner being.

This kind of connection doesn't come from effort or force. You don't have to earn it. It comes when you become still. When you choose presence. When you pause long enough to listen inward.

## STRATEGIES IN THIS PRINCIPLE

3. **Quiet the Noise in Your Head**: You'll learn practical ways to "catch and release" the constant swirl of thoughts, expectations, and distractions—so you can turn down the volume of the world and tune into yourself—and be still.

4. **Trust Your Intuition and Wisdom**: Once the noise fades, your inner voice becomes clearer. This strategy helps you listen to and trust the wise woman within you and hear your purpose.

But before we move on, I invite you to breathe in one more truth.

## AFFIRMATION

*"When I am still, I feel joy and peace from within and allow my inner voice to speak."*

Your *being* is your greatest ally. It's here—in this pause, in this breath—that your *"I am ..."* becomes visible again. Be with it. Cherish it. Let it lead you toward your next step.

## CHAPTER 14

# Strategy 3: Quiet the Noise in Your Head

When I first began to reflect on what it truly meant to *Awaken*, I found that the loudest thing I had to face wasn't the world around me—it was the noise in my head.

And I'm not alone.

Women I've mentored and coached often express their hesitation when I invite them to explore stillness. I hear:

- "Why would I stop my thinking? That's how I succeed."
- "If I slow down, I might lose my edge."
- "Who even am I without the striving and pushing?"
- "I'm so consumed with work and life—I wouldn't know where to begin."

These aren't excuses. They're honest. They're human.

In fact, less than one-third of the women I interviewed in my research mentioned stillness or breath. Only those who already described themselves as spiritual, grounded, or connected to their inner wisdom spoke about the value of being present.

I wasn't surprised. In most workplaces, we've been trained to value action over awareness. Even women with daily spiritual practices rarely think to bring them into the boardroom. But here's the truth: your inner being belongs at work, too.

Stillness isn't a soft skill—it's a strength.

I'm not saying you need to become a monk or start every meeting with meditation. But what if you could borrow just one moment? What if you could create just a small, quiet space inside your day to pause and reconnect?

That one moment can change everything.

Research backs this up. A meta-analysis in *Perspectives on Psychological Science* on self-talk and sports performance found that positive self-talk significantly enhances motivation, confidence, and task performance.[13]

And when we bring this self-awareness into our leadership, we show up differently. More grounded. More present. More powerful.

*Awakening* starts by choosing to pause. To catch the thoughts, fears, and judgments swirling inside us and give them room to breathe. In this strategy, we'll walk through simple, proven ways to do just that.

## Building Mental Muscles

Even the most confident women wrestle with internal noise. Some manage it more gracefully than others, but almost all of us carry it. These doubts, anxieties, and fears may never fully disappear, but they don't have to define us.

Our goal isn't to silence our thoughts. It's to stop being hijacked by them.

The *Journal of Positive Psychology* found that people who regularly practice mindfulness report a decrease in stress and anxiety and also see better decision-making and stronger focus.[14]

So where do we begin?

With our breath.

### The Breath–Brain Connection

Spiritual traditions have told us for centuries what neuroscience now confirms: breath is a bridge. It connects body and mind, conscious and subconscious. It brings us back to the present moment.

Harvard researcher Dr. Sara Lazar used MRI technology to study the effects of an eight-week mindfulness-based stress reduction program on people brand new to meditation. After just 27 minutes a day of simple mindfulness practice, participants showed increased gray matter in areas of the brain responsible for learning, memory, self-regulation, and perspective-taking.[15, 16]

This isn't just about relaxation. It's about transformation. Stillness doesn't make you soft; it makes you clear. And that clarity gives you the power to lead from your *being*, not just your *doing*.

Some women pray. Some journal or recite scripture. Others chant, practice yoga, or meditate. For me, it starts with a pause and a breath. Inhale deeply. Exhale fully. Let your breath guide you to the here and now. Even 30 seconds of presence can shift everything.

Dr. Rebecca Heiss says, "Your breath is the only thing that connects your conscious and your subconscious mind."[17]

When we breathe consciously, we activate the prefrontal cortex—the part of the brain that helps us choose wisely. We quiet the fear-driven fight-or-flight system and step into empowered awareness.

### Controlling What You Can

The most grounded women I interviewed had one thing in common: they knew how to manage the noise. Whether leading teams or navigating politics, they had learned how to pause before reacting.

Stanford neuroscientist Andrew Huberman explains, "You can't control your heart rate directly. You can't control your adrenals. But you can control your breath—and *that* changes everything."[18]

Two simple ways to control your breath are box breathing and 4-7-8 breathing.

Box breathing—used by elite athletes and Navy SEALs alike—is one of my favorite tools. Inhale for four counts. Hold for four. Exhale for four. Hold for four.

This rhythmic breathing calms your nervous system and gives your mind something to focus on.[19] The breath grounds the body. The count anchors the thoughts.

Another favorite is 4-7-8 breathing. Inhale for four counts, hold for seven, and exhale slowly for eight. It's especially helpful in high-stress moments or when panic hits. You don't need a yoga mat or a silent room. You can do this at your desk, in your car, or during a tense meeting. One deep breath can shift your entire response.

## Diya's Story: Quieting the Noise, One Thought at a Time

For years, Diya lived with a quiet, nagging voice in her head—the voice of imposter syndrome. Despite her accomplishments and intellect, it whispered doubts: *Do I belong here? Am I good enough?*

> **RESEARCH SPOTLIGHT**
>
> "I started trying several mindfulness tecniques and becoming more present, especially when my brain is going in a thousand different directions and I have no answers. All I can do is live in this moment. So, that's one way I handle pressure. But I think the most important thing is that I've learned to let go a little bit. A tiny bit, not quite fully."
>
> ~ **Diya | Vice President of Product**

But as we worked together, something shifted. In the stillness of her reflection—through walks, journaling she didn't enjoy but tried anyway, mindfulness, and long solo drives—Diya began to turn the volume down. She learned not to fight the noise, but to listen, acknowledge it, and let it pass.

Bit by bit, she started trusting herself. She stopped striving to prove herself and instead focused on being present—at home, at work, and within.

Her mantra now? "Let go a little. You don't have to be in the driver's seat all the time."

Diya's power isn't loud. It's resilient, intentional, and deeply rooted in self-awareness. One quiet thought at a time, she's rewriting her story. And she's helping others do the same.

Your thoughts can be noisy, but they do not define you. They're stories—some true, some not. As you grow in awareness, you can learn to hold them lightly. Notice. Pause. Breathe. Choose.

Once you begin to take control of your breath and your *being*, you begin to take hold of the incredible power within you. Each thought you catch is an opportunity to practice. Each mindful breath leads you to the space and stillness where you can catch the noise and release it.

This is the path to *Awakening*.

And every breath is an invitation.

To be *SelfPowered*, you must return to yourself.

**CHAPTER 15**

# Strategy 4: Trust Your Intuition and Wisdom

We often talk about our careers like they're supposed to follow a perfect, upward path—a steady climb from one success to the next. But that's not how life works. And it's definitely not how mine unfolded.

The research confirmed what I already knew deep down: most women don't follow a straight line. We rise, we fall, we hit plateaus or pivot completely. Sometimes we leap forward, and sometimes we start over. I've lived that.

There were seasons where my purpose felt crystal clear, like when I was launching Strategy Meets Action, building teams, and influencing an industry.

And then there were times I questioned everything; after leaving Liberty Mutual, after the panic attacks, and even after the success. Those weren't detours. They were turning points. Each one asked me to stop, listen, and trust something deeper in myself.

If we pay attention, those moments, the ones that shake us or stretch us, are often the very places where our truest voice begins to speak. Not the voice of titles or expectations. The voice of your wise woman within.

That's where real alignment—and real power—begins.

A female executive once told me life comes in thirds. The first third, up to age 30, is about becoming: learning, stretching, chasing opportunity. The last third, 60 onward, is about meaning: mentoring, reflecting, giving back.

But it's the middle third that's the grind. Careers, kids, mortgages, aging parents, and endless demands. For me, this third looked like always moving, always achieving, rarely stopping to pause.

That's why learning to listen inward matters. Without it, you can spend decades grinding through a life that no longer fits.

What I've realized is this: we don't want to spend our time just *surviving*. We want to live. We want to feel joy, presence, and connection. To do that, we have to pause, listen, and lead from within.

This strategy is about *Trusting* the voice that lives under the noise—the one that's always been there. Your inner being. Your wise woman. Your intuition.

When you move from *doing* to *being*, your actions start aligning with what truly matters. You don't just react—you respond from a grounded place. You live with clarity and intention, not just achievement.

I love how Indra Nooyi says it: "Figure out what fuels your joy, and you will have found your purpose."[20] That's what your inner voice leads you to—your joy, your purpose, your truth. But to hear her, you need to embrace her. And to embrace her, you need stillness.

Sometimes, she speaks in quiet moments, like when you're sipping your first cup of coffee or walking alone. I call it "morning clarity"—that sudden, quiet knowing. It's not always logical, but it's wise. That's your inner compass.

And like any relationship, trust takes time. You build it by listening, honoring what you hear, and acting on it. That's how you unlock your deepest power.

## Why Are You Here?

Let's talk about purpose. When I ask women this question, most respond with a title or a task: "I'm here to lead a team," or "I solve problems and drive results." That's great—but it's not your purpose.

A few women in the study shared a deeper why—to serve, to influence, to innovate. These were the women who felt most at peace. Most aligned. Most *SelfPowered*.

I believe each of us is here for a reason. I know I am. When I stepped away from chasing the next title and reconnected with my *why*, everything changed. At first, it was about providing for my family and breaking generational patterns. Today, it's about mentoring women and about being a voice of truth and clarity in a world full of noise.

Your purpose might express itself through your work, but it's not just the work. It's your impact. Your *why*.

One mentee of mine said, "But Deb, I love achieving. I don't want to let that go." And I get it—I do too. But achievement isn't the fuel. It's the result. Purpose is the fuel.

When I made that shift, I worried I'd lose my edge. I didn't. I gained vision. I grew a business, sold it, wrote a book, and now I get to share this message with thousands and even millions of women across the globe. The success came—not because I chased it, but because I aligned with my truth.

## What Happens If We Get Off Track?

Let me remind you—*SelfPowerment* isn't about having a flawless track record. It's about learning how to come back to yourself.

It's not a map to a destination. It's a tool to help you find and keep alignment through the evolving seasons of your life and career.

Even when you're grounded in purpose, life can throw you off course. A job loss, a new opportunity, burnout, or a difficult season can cloud your view. Success is not about never drifting. It's about learning to notice the drift and course-correct with clarity and grace. You don't just bounce back—you recalibrate.

Let me show you what this looks like in real life.

### Lauren's Story: Pressing Pause

Lauren is a brilliant executive at a tech startup. We first met in 2020 while working together on a research project. At the time, she was in a season of unexpected transition. Her previous company had downsized, and her position was eliminated. The goal she had been climbing toward suddenly disappeared.

That kind of detour can rattle anyone. It leaves you questioning your value, your direction—even your identity. Lauren had built her career on hard work and persistence. Fresh out of college during the dot-com bubble burst, she took the first job she could find that required a degree. Raised with the belief that perseverance was the key to success, she climbed the corporate ladder without stopping to ask whether she truly loved the work.

Even after she landed a leadership role at a Fortune 500 company, she carried the weight of self-doubt and unfulfilled expectations. She was constantly overextended, juggling high-stakes projects and tight deadlines with little room to breathe. The pressure was constant, and it took a toll on her health and joy.

But when her role was eliminated, Lauren made a courageous choice. She paused. She gave herself space to reflect on her story—who she was, what mattered, and what drove her forward. In working with a therapist and doing deep personal reflection, she realized she had spent years chasing external validation—from her family, her leaders, even the wider business culture. Her career had been impressive but not always aligned.

Lauren began to speak words of courage and affirmation to herself: I am enough. I add incredible value, and even on days where I don't, I am a human, and I am enough as I am.

Over time, she set clearer boundaries, invested in activities that brought her joy, and reconnected with her strengths and values. Slowly, she began making decisions that honored her inner wisdom—not just external expectations.

Lauren learned to listen to her inner voice. And in the process, she rose—not just with success, but with confidence, wisdom and purpose. As a result, her career path had a significant pivot, shifting from a large corporation to a tech startup executive role. And Lauren is not looking back.

## Maria's Story: Tending to Her Path

Maria's story is different. Her turning point didn't come from a loss. It came from a decision—a moment where she had to choose alignment over expectation.

Resilient and determined, Maria had built an extraordinary career. As a Hispanic American woman in business, she faced both subtle and overt challenges—and rose anyway. When a new opportunity to take a top executive role came her way, everyone was surprised that she hesitated. From the outside, it looked like the perfect next step. But inside, Maria felt the tension. *Am I crazy not to do this?* she asked herself. *Think of the good I could do for the community of minority women in business.*

The voices of expectation were loud. But Maria had learned to listen more closely to the quieter voice within. She recognized that her impulse to say yes was fueled by pressure, not peace.

So, she turned to her grounding rituals—her faith, her garden, the quiet spaces where she could reconnect with herself. Tending the soil in her garden had always brought her clarity. And in that stillness, her inner wisdom rose to the surface.

She chose the path that aligned

> **RESEARCH SPOTLIGHT**
>
> "I've learned to define success for myself—not let society define it—and to stay grounded in what truly matters."
>
> **~ Maria | Vice President of Operational Excellence**

with her purpose and honored her passion. One that allowed her to lead not from obligation, but from purpose.

Today, she's not just content; she's thriving and has ended up getting a promotion that aligns with what she's most passionate about—mentoring others, nurturing her team, and leading organizational transformation with intention. Her strength didn't come from chasing what was expected. It came from trusting what felt right for who she was.

To be *SelfPowered*, you must trust your intuition—and follow it.

# PRINCIPLE TWO: Awaken Your Inner Being

*A*wakening begins when we stop striving long enough to hear the quiet voice within. It asks us to pause, breathe, and reconnect—not with titles or tasks, but with who we truly are.

In this principle, you explored what it means to live from stillness. You reflected on the difference between the noise in your head and the awareness beneath it. You learned that presence is not weakness—it's wisdom. It's where your power begins.

The third strategy, *Quiet the Noise in Your Head*, offered tools to help you break free from the constant swirl of demands, expectations, and fear. Through breathwork, reflection, and mindfulness, you began to build new pathways to peace and clarity.

Then, in the fourth strategy, *Trust Your Intuition and Wisdom*, you were invited to listen more deeply—to that wise inner voice that's always been there, gently guiding you back to your purpose.

The stories of Lauren and Maria reminded us that clarity doesn't always come in the form of logic or approval. Sometimes it whispers. And sometimes it asks us to choose alignment over expectation. Your wise woman within already knows. Your job is to listen—and trust her.

Together, these strategies help you step off the hamster wheel of proving, and step into the grounded clarity of *being*. They remind you that you already hold wisdom. You simply need to make space for it to rise.

## ACTION

Create a quiet pause in your day, even just five minutes, and learn to sit in stillness. Breathe deeply. Activate your senses beyond breathing to quiet the mind, for example: feel a warm cup of coffee, smell its aroma, and focus on the burst of flavor of the coffee. This is just a sensory experience. No need to use words or thoughts to describe what you sense.

## STRATEGIES IN THIS PRINCIPLE

3. Quiet the Noise in Your Head
4. Trust Your Intuition and Wisdom

## AFFIRMATIONS

*"I am still. I am aware. I am enough."*

*"I trust the wisdom that rises from within."*

*"When I am still, I feel joy and peace from within and allow my inner voice to speak."*

## PAUSE, REFLECT, REALIGN

- What noises in your head have been on repeat mode? What story are you replaying in your mind? Can you pause and notice it right now—with honesty and curiosity? Can you acknowledge the noise, catch it, hold it, and release it with love and gratitude? As you release it, can you begin to feel an inner shift?

- When was the last time you truly sat in stillness, without solving, striving, or planning? Have you ever noticed that space between your thoughts? What does that stillness feel like to you, and when do you experience it the most?

- If your breath could speak with the wisdom of your inner being, what truth would it reveal about how you are living and showing up in this season of your life?
- What brings you a quiet sense of joy, peace, or wonder, something that feels like you beneath all the doing? What would it mean to follow the inner voices of intuition and wisdom more often? How can you intentionally listen more often to hear your true purpose?

## CHAPTER 16

# PRINCIPLE THREE: Accept the Moment

"The present moment is where your power lies.
Stop chasing and start embracing what is."
**~ Gabby Bernstein**

A s she walked toward the beach, Alex checked her messages one last time. She turned her phone to focus mode—her family could still reach her, but everything else was off-limits.

She pulled her heavy sweater tighter as she stepped into the cool coastal night.

She'd nearly talked herself out of attending the annual Trizenix women's retreat. With finance asking for updated sales projections, a new dashboard review suddenly added to her schedule, and the silent expectation to stay front and center during a critical growth season, she had every reason to stay home.

But then came a text from Renée. Two simple words: "Come anyway."

Now, standing in the salty air under a star-strewn sky, Alex was grateful she had listened, especially since this would probably be the last retreat with Renée.

Renée had just announced her official retirement. Although everyone had known it was coming due to the reorganization, it still came as a shock. Renée was the heartbeat of the culture at Trizenix. She'd been more than a mentor; she had been a mirror, a challenger, and a steady presence.

This retreat had always been more than a perk. It was a symbol of what made Trizenix different. Every woman, from interns to senior leaders, was invited. It was Renée's legacy, a space to connect, reflect, and breathe.

For three days, they shared stories, laughed over wine and good meals, attended workshops, and walked the coastal cliffs. It was rare to see a business so attuned to the personal growth of its people.

Alex stood alone now on one of those cliffs, her cardigan pulled tight as the wind swirled around her. Below, the ocean moved in its slow, steady rhythm. Nature never rushed.

She closed her eyes and inhaled deeply. For the first time in weeks, there was no buzz, no ping, no pull. Her phone was quiet. Her mind, finally, was too.

It felt strange, not being urgently needed.

But it also felt like freedom.

Eventually, she made her way back to the fire pit where the others were gathering.

Renée was already seated, passing out mugs of hot chocolate poured from a thermos. "You look like someone who's finally breathing," she said with a knowing smile, holding out a cup.

"Is it that obvious?" Alex asked as she took the ceramic mug and wrapped her hands around it for warmth.

Renée nodded. "This selection process and all that has changed around here has been a grind. You've been carrying so much on your shoulders. I can see it."

Alex looked down, realizing how tense her shoulders had become.

"I just ... I thought if I worked harder, showed up everywhere, said all the right things, I'd prove I was ready for the CSO role," she said. "But now I'm starting to wonder if the role itself is what I really want or just what I've been chasing."

Renée sipped her drink. "Then maybe stop."

"Stop?"

"Stop trying to win their game. Start asking if it's still your game."

They sat in silence for a long while, the fire crackling between them.

Finally, Alex spoke. "I'm scared they'll choose James."

"And?"

"I'm scared that maybe ... I'll let them."

Renée leaned in gently. "You don't have to prove yourself to anyone, Alex. But you do owe yourself answers. Do you still want this? Or are you just afraid not to want it?"

Alex stared into the flames, letting the words settle.

That night, back in her room, she opened her journal again.

She drew two columns.

| What I Can't Control | What I CAN Control |
|---|---|
| X Whether they chose me | ✓ How I Show Up |
| X The opinions in the board Room | ✓ What I believe about myself |
| X How James is perceived | ✓ What I say yes to |
| X The future | ✓ If I truly want this Role |

She tapped her pen against the page. Then turned to a fresh one and wrote:

> *I don't have to figure it all out tonight.*
> *It's okay to sit with the questions for a while.*
> *When I do choose, I want it to come from what feels right, not from pressure.*

She read the words again and let out a long, steady sigh.

They didn't solve anything, but they felt honest—something she could finally say to herself and feel at peace with.

\* \* \*

## The Freedom of Acceptance

When we truly accept the present moment, something powerful happens. We release the grip of past regrets and stop spinning in the worry of what's next. We let go of what we can't control, and that alone can feel like a deep exhale.

*Acceptance* isn't giving up. It's choosing to meet reality with grace and honesty. It's saying, "This is where I am right now," and holding ourselves accountable for the choices we *can* make.

When we do that, we start to see things differently. We lift our heads. We open our hearts. And we begin to see infinite possibilities.

We begin to make bolder, clearer decisions—ones that align not just with what we do, but with who we truly are.

That's where the freedom is.

When we empower ourselves to make bold, honest decisions, we align our doing with our human-*being*.

## Creating Space

For much of my life, I believed the key to success was in planning ahead— setting goals, managing expectations, staying two steps ahead.

I was a taskmaster, a planner, a doer, and always focused on what was next. I thought if I could just stay organized and in control, I could shape the outcome, avoid missteps, sidestep pain, and secure the career achievements I had worked so hard for.

Unlike some, I didn't dwell on the past. While certain experiences might linger for a day or two, I had a knack for releasing them and moving forward quickly.

But the truth is, no matter how well you and I plan or prepare, life unfolds on its own terms. And whatever is happening in the moment— whether we like it or not, whether it fits the plan or not—it starts with *Acceptance*.

It's easy to get swept away by the noise in your mind: the stories you tell yourself, the emotional undercurrents that pull you off center. But real power lies in your ability to pause, notice, and return—to bring yourself gently back to the here and now.

Because in that moment of *Acceptance*, you create space. And in that space, you find freedom.

*Acceptance* is not giving up. It's simply choosing to stop fighting what *is*.

It's about being honest with yourself, taking ownership of what you can control, learning to let go of the rest, and doing so with compassion.

When you accept the present moment just as it is, you unlock a quieter kind of strength. One that softens the grip, helps you breathe a little easier, and gives you the power of choice to move forward with intention.

I'll never forget the day my executive coach drew a simple chart on the whiteboard in my office. It looked basic—two intersecting lines representing time and space. What she described started another inner shift.

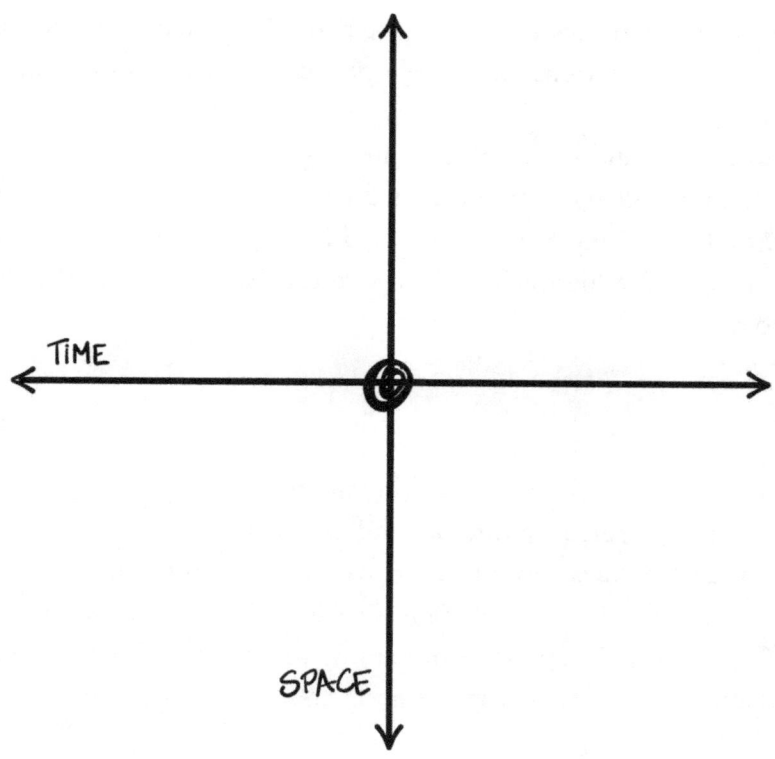

She explained how the center is the present moment, how we often allow our mental energy—the noise in our heads—to pull us out of the moment. Disappointment and guilt take us to the past, or fear and stress take us to the future (time).

And listening to either the words and expectations of others or our own thoughts and emotions pulls us away from our true self (space).

These two forces pull us out of the present in four different directions, sometimes more than one.

For the first time, I began to see that my primary focus had been entirely external, centered on work and others. I was constantly pulled to the future, proving, achieving, and trying to control results. Every day, this created levels of frustration. My worry about future outcomes was the root of my stress and anxiety. It didn't help that I also wasn't being accountable to my own well-being, needs, or growth.

In that moment, I saw myself caught in the mental noise of every corner of the chart; always proving, striving, frustrated with others, second-guessing my actions, and rarely *present*. I was exhausted and filled with anxiety.

This became another turning point in my life.

That simple sketch would eventually become one of the key *SelfPowerment* tools (the InnerShift Map) that I've refined over the years to help women, especially high achievers, locate themselves and find their way back to center.

* * *

When you're at the center of the chart—in the present moment—you're no longer ruled by internal and external pressures and emotions. You're grounded. Clear. Aware. *That's* where your real power lies.

*Honoring* what is, is one of the most essential actions to create an inner shift. On the map, it represents our ability to step out of reactive patterns and return to the center where presence, choice, and clarity live.

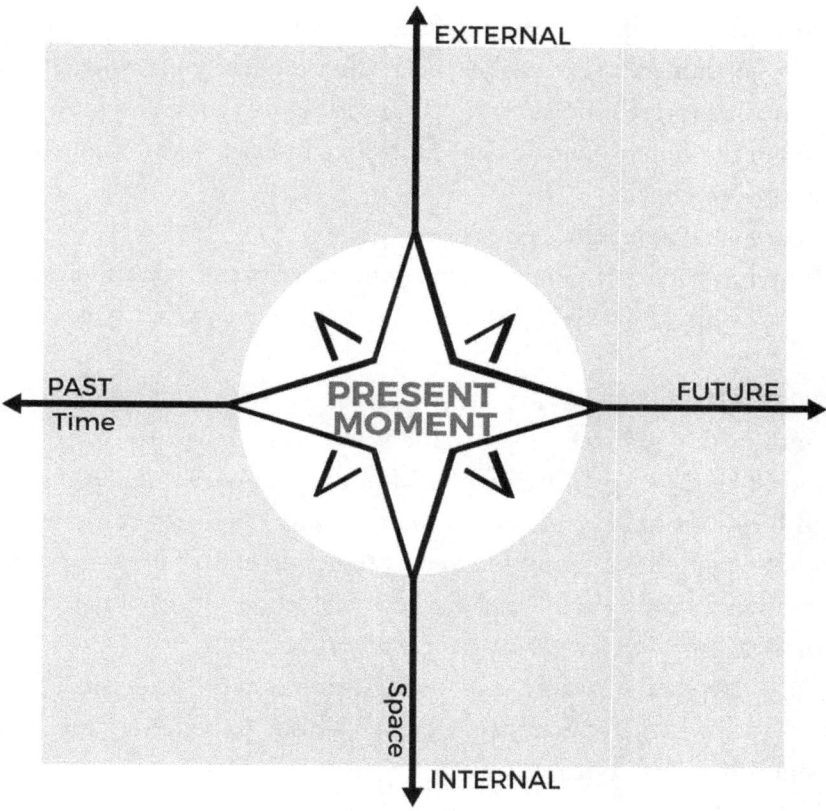

When we're caught in regret about the past or anxiety about the future, we're pulled out of alignment. But when we honor what is, we allow ourselves to gently release resistance and come back to the here and now.

It's a posture of surrender, not in weakness, but in wisdom, a way of reclaiming your energy and stepping into your power with both feet on the ground. This single act of seeing the moment for what it is and meeting it with compassion creates the space that makes the shift possible.

When we resist our circumstances—our emotions, challenges, or experiences—we create tension. We prolong suffering. We keep ourselves stuck in cycles that steal our joy. As Carl Jung said, "What you resist, persists. What you accept, transforms."

The InnerShift Map visually shows this truth. When your thoughts are stuck in the past, you often fall into self-judgment or victimhood.

When you're overwhelmed by the future, anxiety and self-doubt creep in. If you're consumed by external expectations, you lose your voice. If you're stuck in your internal noise, you may second-guess your every move.

But at the center—where time and space intersect—you find stillness, presence, and choice.

That's what *Acceptance* gives you.

It invites you to stop outsourcing your peace to the next milestone and return to yourself. To say: *I am here. This is what is. Now what do I choose?*

## LIVING IT OUT

Integrating this practice into my life wasn't easy. I had to let go of old wounds, like the sting of leaving KPMG. I had to release the grip of *what if* and begin grounding myself in *what is*. And I had to wrestle with the safety of staying in a secure job versus the courage to follow my calling. My mother's words about financial security echoed in my head, but my inner voice grew louder: *This is your moment.*

So, I stepped forward. Not recklessly, but with grounded faith. I trusted that when I operate from center—from presence—I make decisions not from fear, but from truth.

This is the power of *Acceptance*.

It frees you from false timelines, from other people's scripts, and from the pressure to always have it figured out. It allows you to live in the present, not just plan for the future. It creates space for dreaming, for breathing, for *being*.

And it leads to two powerful questions:
- *Am I accepting of what is happening right now?*
- *What can I release so I can return to the present moment?*

As author and speaker Gabby Bernstein says, "The present moment is where your power lies. Stop chasing and start embracing what is."[21]

That's what the next two strategies will help you explore.

## STRATEGIES IN THIS PRINCIPLE

5. **Honor What Is**: By embracing the present, we can experience life fully as it unfolds without resistance.

6. **Own Your Actions and Choices**: By being accountable, you can live your life and career with purpose.

*Acceptance* isn't passive. It's active. It's not about settling. It's about accepting your life with grace, courage, and clarity. So, take a breath. Right here. Right now.

## AFFIRMATION

*"I honor what is and accept the moment as if it were designed for me."*

This is where your *SelfPowerment* takes root. This is where everything begins to shift.

## CHAPTER 17

# Strategy 5: Honor What Is

There's a quiet kind of strength that comes from letting go. Not giving up but releasing the need to control every outcome. *Honoring* what is means choosing to stop fighting the moment you're in and, instead, meet it with grace and curiosity.

This isn't something I learned in a single moment. It's something I've practiced for years—sometimes with intention, sometimes only in hindsight.

I honored what was when I chose to leave Liberty Mutual, even though it felt scary. I eventually accepted what came when KPMG asked me to resign (even though I had known deep down it wasn't a fit, I stayed longer than I should have for the title and the money).

I honored what was again when I left TowerGroup to launch Strategy Meets Action. And when it was time to sell that business, I leaned into that moment with acceptance and grace, even though it was bittersweet.

I've learned that life doesn't always follow the plan I expect. Even the best strategy can be disrupted. But if you can meet the moment rather than resist it, something surprising happens. Clarity arrives.

Clarity doesn't always come in the form of a solution or next step. Sometimes, it's simply peace. Sometimes, it's releasing the breath you didn't realize you'd been holding. Sometimes, it's paying attention to the soft voice inside that says, *This is not the end. This is a beginning.*

*Honoring* what is doesn't mean we stop dreaming. It means we stop struggling. It's a practice—a gentle surrender to reality without abandoning our desire to grow. It's how we make space for wisdom, healing, and new direction.

For me, this practice shows up in both big life decisions and tiny, daily moments. When plans change, when people disappoint, when things break, or when I'm standing in a long line at Trader Joe's, feeling rushed and irritated.

I breathe. I pause. And I whisper, *What if this is happening for me? What if I accepted this as if I had chosen it?*

That small shift opens a door to something greater.

## Kate's Story: The Power of Accepting What Is

Kate had built a thriving career as an executive in financial services. Known for her drive and intelligence, she was on a fast track and by age 40, she had achieved what many only dreamed of. But life had a different plan. After narrowly missing a flight from Boston to LA on 9/11, a plane she was regularly on, she was jolted into a moment of clarity.

Around the same time, her daughter was diagnosed with autism spectrum disorder. It became clear: something in her life needed to shift.

She felt paralyzed at first. How could she keep up with her career ambition and also meet the changing needs of her family? Things became clear to her once she looked at the moment authentically and realized her life season had changed right in front of her.

She embraced the reality of what was.

"I just need to go home," she told me. "No one's going to care for my daughter better than me."

Stepping away from the corporate world wasn't just about her family; it was a bold act of honoring herself. But in choosing to accept the moment as it was, not as she wished it would be, Kate found freedom. She redirected her career energy into community leadership, joining the board of the local bank and staying connected to the business world on *her* terms.

Twelve years later, her daughter went off to college. Kate felt the pull to return to corporate leadership. Despite doubts—both internal and external—she chose to believe in her worth. Her return wasn't about picking up where she left off; it was about stepping forward as a *SelfPowered* woman, deeply rooted in purpose and experience.

Kate's story is a powerful reminder that *Acceptance* is not resignation—it's strength. She didn't walk away from ambition; she expanded its meaning. In choosing to honor what *was*, Kate created space for what *could be*. Her journey reflects the very heart of *SelfPowerment*: trusting the moment, honoring your truth, and making bold choices that align with your being.

* * *

Not every woman will respond the same way to family versus career decisions. How we accept the moment and make the bold choices are all personal, unique, and complex. There is no right or wrong response.

Again and again, I've heard stories of women who have chosen to honor what is. Women who faced discrimina-

> **RESEARCH SPOTLIGHT**
> "Being in the moment
> is when you're doing something and
> you're not thinking about the past,
> you're not thinking about the future,
> you're not thinking about worries …
> you're just experiencing."
> **~ Jasmine | Managing Director**

tion, exclusion, or betrayal and chose not to carry the weight of what they couldn't change.

They stopped resisting. Some women chose to leave the company, not out of bitterness, but from a place of peace. Other women decided to stay, but with a new perspective. And in this act of *Acceptance*, they reclaimed their power.

That's what this strategy offers you.

It doesn't mean settling. It means softening. It means showing up for your life as it is—with clarity, courage, and compassion.

Because when you stop tugging at the moment, life begins to flow. And it flows toward your highest good.

Let's begin by asking:

- *What am I holding onto that I could release?*
- *Where am I resisting reality, and how could I meet it instead?*
- *What if this moment, as imperfect as it feels, is here to teach me something?*

This is how you reclaim your energy.

This is how you return to center.

This is what it means to be *SelfPowered*.

To be *SelfPowered*, you must let go and meet the moment with open hands and an open heart.

## CHAPTER 18

# Strategy 6: Own Your Actions and Choices

For most of my career, I took pride in my accountability. I delivered results. I kept commitments. I did the hard things—usually without complaint.

Whether for my teams, my leaders, my clients, or my family, I carried the weight with strength and grace. But somewhere in all of that responsibility, I forgot one crucial thing: I was accountable to everyone but myself.

That blind spot came into sharp focus one day in one of my executive coaching sessions. I was venting about the usual things: people missing deadlines, lack of follow-through by others, the weight of having to carry so much.

My executive coach listened quietly, then simply said, "Now, point that finger back at yourself."

It stopped me cold. She was right. I had been holding others to a standard I wasn't fully living by. Not just in the office, but in my personal life.

I was accountable to my family, to my daughters, to my husband, to my mother, to my boss, to my team, to my customers, to the company I worked for. And not accountable to *me* at all.

I was putting myself last. My body was suffering. My energy was depleted. I wasn't doing anything that fed my soul. I had lost sight of what *I* needed, because I was so focused on everything and everyone else.

That moment marked another turning point. I realized that true accountability isn't just about performance or outcomes—it's about alignment. It's about honoring your own needs, your truth, your voice. It's about choosing the life and work that reflect who you really are.

So, I began the work. I started prioritizing my well-being. I set new boundaries. I made new choices. I got healthy—emotionally, physically, spiritually. And from that place of clarity, I made one of the boldest moves of my career: I left TowerGroup and launched Strategy Meets Action.

That decision wasn't just a business move—it was an act of radical accountability. I stopped waiting for someone else to give me permission. I chose myself. And I've never looked back.

Amelia Earhart is one of the most courageous and brave women in modern history. She truly lived a *SelfPowered* life. Her words deeply resonate with the importance of this strategy, "The most difficult thing is the decision to act—the rest is merely tenacity."[22]

Once I made the decision to act, the momentum carried me forward. Because action, when it's aligned, creates energy.

*Owning* your actions and choices is one of the most powerful expressions of *SelfPowerment*. It means:

- You stop outsourcing your authority.
- You stop waiting for clarity to be handed to you.
- You trust yourself to decide—and then move.

## Reclaiming Accountability to You

*Owning* your choices doesn't mean you have to have it all figured out. It means you stop handing over the pen. You stop asking for permission to make a change, to speak up, to slow down, or to take a leap. You start living and leading from your center.

Sometimes this looks like saying no to something that's "fine" but not aligned. Sometimes just because you *can* does not mean you *should*.

Sometimes it means risking disappointment or judgment to stay true to what matters most. But it always means choosing from within.

"Don't let others define you. You define yourself," says Ginni Rometty, the first female CEO of IBM."[23]

That's what it looks like to own your actions and choices. To act not out of fear or habit, but out of self-trust. That's when real *Alignment* takes root.

## Real Women, Real Wisdom

Through my research, one truth surfaced again and again: women want to live and lead on their own terms but often struggle to make choices that honor themselves.

The 52 women shared stories of burnout, over-functioning, and silent resentment. Stories of staying too long in roles that no longer fit, driven by obligation, fear, or financial reasons. But alongside the struggle came turning points, moments of clarity when they finally said, *"Enough. I choose me."*

As one woman reflected, "It's full ownership of your roles and being accountable to yourself."

These women didn't just talk about balance. They made bold, and sometimes difficult, choices rooted in *Alignment*.

## Lindsay's Story: Leading with Choice, Not Guilt

When a critical business meeting was scheduled on the same day as her son's pre-school field day, Lindsay faced a moment that many working mothers know all too well. The tension between presence at home and responsibility at work pulled at her. But rather than let guilt make the decision, she paused and applied Suzy Welch's 10-10-10 framework,[24] asking: *How will this feel in 10 minutes? Ten months? Ten years?*

In 10 minutes, she knew she'd feel torn. In 10 months, she'd still be proud of showing up fully in her role. And in 10 years? Her son probably wouldn't even remember missing the school event. But she would remember the opportunity she said yes to the decision that helped shape her career.

Other moms raised their eyebrows. Some questioned her priorities. But Lindsay was confident in her choice. She lovingly communicated with her son that both his father and grandparents were going to be at the field day, and showed up for her executive meeting with strength, and honored what mattered in that moment for her.

"You can't be afraid to be a parent at work, and you can't be afraid to be a worker when you're at home—because both are a part of you," Lindsay shared.

That day, she didn't choose work over family—she chose *Alignment* over approval. She modeled for her children what courage, clarity, and self-defined success look like.

### RESEARCH SPOTLIGHT

"Every woman has the potential to lead and succeed. It's about making the right choices and having the courage to pursue your goals. The power of choice always resides within you."

**~ Sharon | Board Director & Retired Global Managing Director**

Her story is a powerful reminder that *SelfPowerment* doesn't mean always getting it right. It means getting it *true*—making the decisions that reflect your deepest values and owning them.

That's *SelfPowerment*. That's what it looks like to accept the present moment and make bold choices grounded in who you are, with your purpose.

To be *SelfPowered*, you must own your choices, act on them, and trust your inner voice.

# PRINCIPLE THREE: Accept the Moment

A*cceptance* begins when we stop resisting long enough to notice what's already here. It doesn't mean we give up or give in; it means we wake up. To the moment. To our truth. To our power.

In this principle, you explored what it means to come home to *now*. You reflected on how the past can tug at your heart, and how fear of the future can pull you out of your power. But when you return to the present, you reconnect with your *"I am ... "* Not the woman others expect you to be, but the woman you already are.

The fifth strategy, *Honor What Is*, invited you to soften into this moment, no matter how imperfect or uncertain. You began to loosen your grip on what you can't control and made peace with what is, as if it were designed for you.

The story of my own acceptance—from corporate transition to personal growth—offered my real-world view of how surrender can lead to strength.

Then, in the sixth strategy, *Own Your Actions and Choices*, you were called to reclaim accountability—not just to roles and responsibilities but to yourself. You discovered that living aligned with your values means honoring your well-being, your needs, and your voice.

Lindsay's story showed that courageous decisions don't always make sense to others, but they do have meaning for you.

Together, these strategies offer more than coping; they offer clarity. They remind you that every moment, no matter how messy, is an opportunity to show up with grace and courage.

This is what it means to be *SelfPowered*: not perfect, but present. Not in control, but in alignment. Not proving, but choosing.

## ACTION

Choose one place where you've been resisting reality. Pause, breathe, and ask: What would it feel like to accept this moment fully—and act from there? Why am I holding onto it?

## STRATEGIES IN THIS PRINCIPLE

5. Honor What Is
6. Own Your Actions and Choices

## AFFIRMATIONS

"I meet the moment with grace and strength."

"I trust the present to show me my next step."

"I honor what is and accept the moment as if it were designed for me."

## PAUSE, REFLECT, REALIGN

- What part of your current reality have you been resisting, one that might create an inner shift if you accept it as if it were designed for you and your growth?
- Where in your life have you been accountable to others before yourself? What would it feel like to choose differently and start with your being first?
- What bold choice are you being invited to make but haven't because of fear, guilt, or loyalty to an outdated version of yourself?

- How fully present are you most days? What are the noises pulling you out of the present moment? When you are present, pay attention to what aligns within you.

## CHAPTER 19

# PRINCIPLE FOUR: Align Your Doing

"Authenticity is the daily practice of letting go of who we think
we're supposed to be and embracing who we are."
**~ Brené Brown**

Alex paced slowly in front of her home office desk. Her grandmother's clock chimed from the hallway—11:00 p.m.

She stopped. Took a breath. Then turned back to her laptop. Both PowerPoint windows were still open, side by side.

On the left was the polished corporate deck: 14 slides of tightly crafted metrics, strategic frameworks, and precise lingo. She'd been refining it for weeks.

On the right was something entirely different: just four slides, clean and simple. *"Power in Connection: Building Sales Cultures That Last."* She had built it in the last hour, shaping it with her voice, her team's insights, and none of the corporate fluff—only what truly mattered, alignment.

This was it. Tomorrow was the final pitch for the CSO position. She and James were the only candidates being considered for the role.

Alex hovered the mouse over the corporate-sounding version on the left. Then, she made a decision. Without flinching, she pressed delete. It felt good.

She had spent too long performing, adapting, and perfecting. Now, she wanted to show up as herself.

For the first time in a long while, she wasn't preparing for approval. She was preparing to show up fully as herself, confident in who she was.

Alex walked to the back of her closet to get her clothes out for the next day.

There it was: her red blazer. The one she wore when she landed the big McLaren deal. The blazer she hadn't touched in months. She reached for it, knowing it was the right choice.

This wasn't a shield to protect her. It was a reminder of who she already was.

The next morning, she sat at her desk sipping coffee, being still, fully aware of the deep rich aroma, the warmth of the cup on her hands, the taste of her favorite hazelnut flavor. She steadied herself for the meeting ahead. She was ready.

As she stood and slid her notes into her portfolio, a red envelope slipped off the corner of her desk. Handwritten on the front were just two words: *To Alex.*

She opened it carefully. The card showed a soft watercolor of the ocean. Inside, in the blank white space, were just a few handwritten words:

*We see you. You already lead us.*

*- The Team*

A lump rose in her throat. Her people had shown up for her. They stayed, worked late, and believed in what they were building together.

Even when she doubted herself, they hadn't. And they hadn't followed her because she was flawless. They followed her because she showed up— real, present, and steady.

That's what she was bringing into the final interview: not a mask, not a performance, but her full, present self.

Alex stood just outside the boardroom, her shoulders without tension, her hands relaxed at her sides, her heart steady and calm.

James walked up in a crisp navy suit. He looked focused and confident. He nodded at her with a respectful smile. She smiled back.

This didn't feel like a showdown anymore. It felt like a moment of truth.

Not, *Will they choose me?* But, *Do I choose this?*

She drew a slow, deep breath.

I'm not here to prove anything, she thought. I'm here to speak clearly, live boldly, and honor who I am.

The door opened. "Alex, we're ready for you."

Shoulders back, head high, she tucked her portfolio under her arm and stepped into the room.

\* \* \*

## The Power of Alignment

In a world that constantly urges us to do more, be more, and prove more, *Alignment* offers a radical truth: you are already enough.

This fourth principle of the *SelfPowerment* Framework is the culmination of everything we've explored so far.

*Alignment* is the integration of who you are with what you do.

It's about the inner shift from striving to thriving, from external validation to internal coherence. It's a move from performance to presence. And the promise is to exchange exhaustion for energy.

To *Align Your Doing* means to step fully into the present moment with intention. It's not about doing more—it's about doing from a place of wholeness. When high-achieving women bring their full being into their human-*doing*, their actions begin to reflect their deeper truth. They lead, speak, and move not just with ambition, but with purpose.

This principle invites us to let go of the autopilot mode so many of us have lived in. To move beyond titles and checklists. To pause and ask: *What truly matters now? What version of success actually feels good to me?*

*Alignment* is not about perfection.

Again, *Align Your Doing* is not about abandoning ambition. It's about fueling it differently—less from self-doubt, more from wisdom. When you operate from *Alignment*, you move from flow, not force. You act with clarity. You create from peace.

And you begin to experience success that not only looks good on the outside but feels good on the inside.

For many high-achieving women, the traditional markers of success—titles, income, influence—have been a roadmap, and we've followed it well. We've climbed, led, built, achieved and delivered. But somewhere along the way, many of us arrive at a silent question: *Is this it?*

It's not that the success wasn't real.

It's that it wasn't complete.

We're not yearning to walk away from ambition—we're yearning to expand what success means. We're craving joy that isn't delayed. Fulfillment that isn't conditional.

To align with your authentic self is to honor your truth over the noise, your purpose over perfection, and your being over relentless doing.

In order to step into *Alignment*, you have to humbly and honestly ask yourself two things:

- *In what ways am I still trying to be who I think I should be?*
- *What would it look like to be more me today?*

When your actions align with your values and your deeper why, you operate in coherence. Studies show that this state boosts resilience, creativity, and leadership effectiveness. But more than that, it restores something even more powerful: your sense of integrity with yourself.

This is not about relinquishing drive; it's about recalibrating it so it serves you rather than drains you. When you stop trying to control outcomes, you start cultivating the conditions for meaningful success.

### Owning Your Presence

When you choose to live in *Alignment*, you begin to own your presence, not to impress others, but to express your truth.

Think back to your answer to the elephant question. When you own your unique strengths and intrinsic leadership style, you allow your authentic presence and purpose to shine through.

Your energy speaks before you say a word—grounded, intentional, and aligned. When you walk into a room, it's not just that people see you, they *feel* your presence.

You begin to speak by leveraging the full range of your voices—not louder, but clearer, and always with intention for the moment. You let your words rise from *Alignment*, choosing the voice that serves the purpose:

- Strategic, as the Wise Woman with vision and discernment
- Operational, as the Taskmaster with clarity and precision
- Empathetic, as the Nurturer with compassion and care, or
- Influential, as the Communicator, using presence and truth to inspire

Each voice has its power.

Use yours with intention, not to impress, but to impact, not for approval, but from confidence, self-worth, and self-love because you've learned to accept the fullness of who you are—not just the polished parts, but the tender, unfinished, and growing parts too.

You've awakened to your inner voice—the one that's always been there, quiet and steady beneath the noise, waiting for you to slow down and listen. It neither shouts nor demands. It gently calls you back to what truly matters—your human-*being*, your vision, your truth. And it reminds you that clarity doesn't come from doing more, but from being more fully present with yourself.

And that changes everything.

## When You Walk into a Room

"How do other people see you when you walk into a room?"

I'll never forget this pivotal question from my executive coach. I paused. Not because I didn't have an answer, but because I had never thought about it that way before.

I had spent years focused on the doing. The delivery. The execution. But rarely had I paused to consider the energy I carried. The presence I exuded. The impact I left.

It was a moment of deep self-reflection that sparked a new, clearer vision.

I began by writing down how I thought others saw me. Calm, experienced, knowledgeable, strategic, in control.

As I delved deeper, I recognized other qualities that I hadn't fully acknowledged in myself. *Warmth, intuition, and a nurturing spirit.* I added how I saw myself. *A figure of stability, someone who knew how to get things done.*

Yet even as I wrote these words, I sensed a gap between who I saw myself to be and the person I aspired to be.

My coach then asked another question that struck even deeper: "What do you want people to see, feel, and hear when you walk into a room?"

It forced me to confront the difference between how I currently showed up and the identity I truly wanted to embody.

I want to be seen as someone with high energy, focus, and power. Sleek, stunning, and classy. A female executive who not only leads but also guides others through any challenge. A woman who moves with intention and lives with purpose. I want to shift my voice from that of an operational taskmaster to that of a strategic wise woman.

That bold vision became my guiding light. It was an intention and an affirmation.

Over the next year, I made the inner shift, aligning with my human-*being*. I invested in my health, hiring a personal trainer and a dietitian. I stopped worrying about what others thought, let go of comparison, and focused on choices that aligned with my strengths and purpose. I walked into rooms with a newfound confidence, at ease with my true self. It wasn't about a physical transformation or a new job title. It was about who I chose to be.

Within a year of writing down how I saw myself and how I wanted others to see me, I had become the female executive I envisioned. I moved to San Diego and assumed a new position as Chief Information Officer and Chief Transformation Officer at the Insurance Company of the West, a privately owned insurance company.

Like a living vision board, I chose my direction. And rather than wanting, waiting, or wishing, I took one step at a time to ultimately manifest my vision.

I continue to grow and evolve, choosing daily to align my true *"I am ... "*

*Alignment* is not a destination. It's one decision, one move, one action at a time in the present moment.

## For Women in Transition

Many of the women leaders I mentor are in a season of career transition. Some by choice, others not. Either way, the question that often emerges isn't, *Can I succeed again?* It's deeper. *Will I ever succeed and still feel like myself?*

*SelfPowerment* becomes a tool in these moments.

You may be in a job that looks great on paper but drains your soul. Or you may be between roles, wondering what's next. You may feel pressure to keep pushing. Or guilt for wanting more.

But *Alignment* isn't about waiting for the perfect next step. It's about choosing to fully show up in the step you're in.

You can be unemployed and still walk in purpose. You can be in a mismatched role and still choose to show up with authenticity.

*Alignment* is not a title. It's a posture.

## Pause and Reflect

- What would it look like to align with your *"I am ... "* today—even if your circumstances haven't caught up yet?
- What's one decision you could make from power, not pressure?
- Where could you speak with your real voice, even in the in-between?

## The Heart of Alignment

Practicing *Alignment* is about more than balance. It's about integrity. Every action, every interaction, every word, is rooted in who you are.

This is your life. No one else can live it. You get to choose the tone. The rhythm. The values. The direction.

*Alignment* isn't a one-time moment of clarity. It's a daily choice of courageous self-honoring. As Brené Brown defines authenticity as "the daily practice of letting go of who we think we're supposed to be and embracing who we are."[25]

Our last two strategies are going to help you put this principle in motion.

### STRATEGIES IN THIS PRINCIPLE

7. **Connect Intentionally**: Genuine connections, founded on authenticity and mutual respect, will become a source of strength and support and will enable you to thrive.
8. **Create Your Future Self**: Now that you've centered yourself with stillness, clarity, and purpose, it's time to step into becoming who you truly are. This strategy invites you to align your choices and actions, not by chasing, but by living from your deepest truth every day forward.

You don't have to earn your worth through doing. Your *"I am ... "* is already enough.

### AFFIRMATION

*"I am ... enough. I choose to live today with purpose and intention, aligned to my human-being."*

When you lead from *Alignment*, you don't just make an impact. You leave a legacy.

## CHAPTER 20

# Strategy 7: Connect Intentionally

Success isn't a solo journey. Behind every powerful woman is a network that fuels her courage, expands her vision, and helps her rise—not just in career, but in confidence, clarity, and connection.

For much of my career, I underestimated the true power of networking. I focused on selling and delivering results, partnering with trusted advisors, and mastering strategy behind the scenes. I had many executive coaches but no community. I was supported but not surrounded.

Looking back, I now see what I was missing: the collective wisdom, energy, and expansion that come from intentionally building a diverse network that both *sees* you and *strengthens* you, and helps lift you up.

Like many of the women I interviewed, I didn't know how to network for career advancement, insights, and role success in the same way as men. And like many women, I often connected for conversation, and occasionally for collaboration. But rarely did I ask for help in my job.

I believed that grit, determination, and independence would be enough.

I now know that living *SelfPowered* is not a solo act. It flourishes in connection. And not just any connection—*intentional connection*.

And even more so, through women helping women.

## From Isolation to Expansion

For years, I operated within my own self-contained system—focused, productive, and outwardly successful. Inwardly, though, I felt isolated. I reached out only when absolutely necessary. All along, I didn't realize the power I was forfeiting by not stepping into a networked way of living and leading.

That all changed when "Deb 2.0" emerged. I became more engaged in an expansive network of women in leadership with diverse backgrounds and experiences. The shift was immediate and profound. The wisdom and energy of other women augmented and fueled the development of *Self-Powerment*.

I was helping and I was learning. I was giving and I was receiving. A new synergy of two-way connection emerged. I experienced growth and being uplifted in ways I had never imagined. And along the way, I learned that asking for help is a reflection of wisdom and strength.

Building intentional relationships isn't optional—it's *essential* to *Self-Powerment*. You can't align your life or leadership if you're isolated. And you can't evolve into your highest self if you're hiding.

## Fueling Success Through Connection

The research is clear:

- Women who intentionally build professional networks are 50% more likely to succeed in their careers.[26]
- Research shows that professionals with diverse networks are significantly more likely to drive innovation and uncover new opportunities.[27]
- And professionals with strong networks report higher career satisfaction, salary, and progression.[28]

This isn't just about knowing people. It's about cultivating meaningful, multidimensional relationships with mentors, peers, communities, and sponsors—people who will help you align with your purpose, power, and potential.

## Authenticity Is the Catalyst

In the *SelfPowerment* journey, intentional connection is the difference between operating from isolation and thriving in *Alignment*. It's about curating your relationships with care—choosing those who reflect your values, support your truth, and celebrate your becoming. Leigh and Nikki, two extraordinary women I interviewed, embody this strategy in different yet authentic ways.

## Leigh's Story: Leading Through Asking

As a CEO of a billion-dollar enterprise, Leigh learned a foundational truth about leadership: you don't have to know everything—you need to know who to ask for help.

"If I don't understand something, I'll call 50 friends until I find someone who can help me figure it out," she shared.

For her, asking for help isn't a weakness; it's a strategy.

Leigh has built an ecosystem around her: advisors, experts, decision-makers, and visionary peers who challenge her thinking and expand her perspective. Her network isn't accidental. It's intentional, woven with wisdom, trust, and alignment. And it's part of what makes her leadership so impactful.

## Nikki's Story: Leading Through Authenticity

Nikki approaches leadership differently. For her, connection begins with showing up fully, vulnerabilities and all.

"When I think about the women I've connected with through events and opportunities, it's not just about professional growth," she shared, "it's about creating a space where we support and lift each other up."

She doesn't build relationships to *impress*, she builds them to connect. Her sincerity creates safety. Her presence builds trust. And that ripple effect of openness and encouragement has made her a magnetic force in every circle she enters.

\* \* \*

Leigh leads through strategy. Nikki leads through sincerity. But both women have one thing in common: their intentional networks uplift themselves and others. Their relationships are rooted in who they *are*, not just what they *do*.

Because real connection doesn't happen at the surface.

It happens when you show up as *you*.

## Build the Network That Reflects Who You're Becoming

The people we choose to connect with are not just companions; they are catalysts. As a self-made billionaire (the founder of Spanx), Sara Blakely frequently emphasizes the importance of being intentional in who you surround yourself with, arguing that the energy and ideas of the right network can significantly amplify your success.[29]

The right relationships can spark innovation, unlock opportunities, and offer the steady support we need to walk boldly into our next chapter. But none of that happens by accident. It takes intentionality.

This is about more than networking. It's about consciously creating a multi-dimensional ecosystem of connection that strengthens both your internal and external power.

To become the woman you're meant to be, you need to surround yourself with people who reflect that future self, who challenge, support, and elevate you. This includes building relationships across multiple levels and layers:

- **Internal**: This includes strategic collaborators, mentors, sponsors, and aligned leadership within your organization, those who offer guidance, open doors, and advocate for your growth. It also includes cross-functional partners or collaborators who help advance your goals.
- **Peers**: These are trusted colleagues, thought partners, and support circles that energize your thinking and challenge your growth—friends, peers, or circles who provide care, empathy, and perspective.

- **External**: Here, the focus is on communities, industry networks, professional advisors, and coaches who expand your visibility and perspective. External experts who help you stay clear, grounded, and aligned to your *"I am ... "*

Connection isn't about collecting contacts. It's about building an ecosystem that reflects the wholeness of your future self and choosing to rise in community, not isolation.

Remember, you weren't meant to do this alone. You are a human-*being*, doing. And your doing becomes more powerful when it's seen, supported, and surrounded.

To be *SelfPowered*, you must build intentionally, connect courageously, and rise—together.

> **RESEARCH SPOTLIGHT**
>
> "My superpower is my networking capabilities– connecting with the people that I love. In this lifetime, my legacy will come from the fact that the connection with people is meaningful and that I am helping people to change their lives."
>
> ~ Mei-Li | Vice President of Analytics

## CHAPTER 21

# Strategy 8: Create Your Future Self

There's a moment—often quiet, sometimes urgent—when you realize that who you've been is not necessarily who you want to become. Not because you've failed, but because you've grown.

This final strategy is your invitation to become the woman you're meant to be. And to do so *on purpose*. Not by default or drift but by conscious design. This is where *Alignment* becomes action, where your *"I am ..."* begins shaping your *"I will ..."*

Creating your future self isn't about chasing a new version of success. It's about becoming more fully *you*—with clarity, conviction, and compassion. And the key isn't out there. It's in the present moment.

When you live aligned with your inner wisdom, your human-*being*, and your unique presence, you're no longer reacting. You're creating. You become the human-*being*, doing—your true self.

And the future you want doesn't start someday.

It starts now, living as if you already are her.

### From Identity to Intention

Who you are becoming is not a mystery; it's a decision. In *SelfPowerment*, you recognize that the future is not something you wait for. It's something you shape. Every thought, every action, every "yes" and every "no" becomes a building block of the life you're creating.

But you can't build a future from exhaustion. Or confusion. Or someone else's blueprint. You build it by showing up whole, awake, present, and letting your human-*being* lead the doing.

## Pause and Reflect

Pause and ask yourself:

- *Who am I becoming?*
- *What do I want to feel more of in my life?*
- *How do I want to show up, lead, and live?*

Your answers won't come all at once. They'll rise from your inner voice as you slow down. As you listen in. And as you trust what you already know.

## Becoming You

Manifesting your future self is not wishful thinking or wishful wanting. It's intentional *Alignment*.

It begins with clarity: seeing your future self not as a far-off fantasy, but as a version of you already forming. When you envision her—how she leads, lives, speaks, and rests—you begin to live from that place. You shift your choices, your posture, and even your energy to align with the future you're calling in.

Manifestation isn't passive. It's active. It's a daily return to the vision of your future self, paired with consistent action and the belief that what you desire is not only possible; it's already unfolding.

This is where *SelfPowerment* meets creation. You're not just reacting to what life brings—you're choosing what to build. By speaking your intentions, visualizing outcomes, and making aligned decisions, you're signaling to yourself and the world: *I am becoming her now.*

Your future self isn't waiting. She's being shaped by every courageous, present-moment choice you make today.

**Envision "You ..."**

Take a moment to imagine your future self.

- *When you walk into a room, how do you want people to see, feel, and hear you?*
- *How do you move through the day?*
- *What kind of energy surrounds you?*
- *What words describe how you live and lead?*

This isn't about titles, roles, or a job description. It's not nouns, but adjectives. Not achievements, but essence. This is about who you are at your core.

You're not creating an idealized fantasy. You're connecting to a version of yourself that already exists—one that's waiting to be invited forward. It's you, more centered. More vibrant. More true.

- Maybe you speak up without hesitation.
- Maybe you stop overexplaining.
- Maybe you take your place—every place—without apology.
- Maybe your mornings are softer, your boundaries fiercer, your decisions bolder.

You don't hustle for worthiness. You live from it.
You are your living vision board.

**The Present Moment Is the Portal**

The only way to meet your future self is to move through the present moment. You don't need to overhaul your life to become her. You simply need to begin making choices that *reflect* her.

Each time you say yes to what's aligned and no to what drains, you draw closer.

Each time you speak honestly, lead boldly, or rest without guilt, you embody her.

Each time you pause, breathe, and listen to your inner voice, you become her.

This is how change happens—not in one sweeping act, but in thousands of quiet, aligned choices.

In fact, research consistently shows that people who live in alignment with their core self-concept report greater life satisfaction, emotional well-being, and a deeper sense of purpose than those who chase achievement alone.[30]

Your future self is not out of reach. She's within you. And she's calling you forward not because you're not enough, but because you're finally ready to be all of you.

## From Alex's Story and Mine

Alex, the woman whose journey you've witnessed unfold through the framework, has reached a turning point. Like many of the women who walk through *SelfPowerment*, she has come to a choice: trying to stay in a role that may no longer fit her or living forward in *Alignment*.

She's no longer trying to play someone else's game. She's listening to her inner voice. She's present. She's clear. And with that clarity comes courage: *I'm not here to prove anything. I'm here to speak clearly, live boldly, and honor who I am.*

> **RESEARCH SPOTLIGHT**
> "Embrace bold choices
> that align with your true self,
> and let each decision open the door
> to new possibilities."
>
> **~ Jan | Chief Executive Officer**

Alex has begun to create from this grounded space. Rather than scrambling for the next opportunity, she's shaping her life with vision and intention.

She's no longer chasing her future. She's becoming it.

And so are you.

When I first wrote down how I wanted to be seen, felt, and heard when I walked into a room, I had no idea how powerful that act would be.

It was more than a wish list. It was a claim. A declaration.

And with every aligned step I took, I not only grew into the woman I wished to be—I became the woman *I am*. Not because I changed who I was, but because I finally allowed myself to *be* her.

I released all guilt and shame and became the deserving woman I believed I am.

That's the power of living with ease and peace. That's the power of aligning your doing with your human-*being*.

You don't have to hustle your way there.

You just have to start choosing and being.

To be *SelfPowered*, you must live who you are becoming.

# PRINCIPLE FOUR: Align Your Doing

When you've awakened, accepted, and reconnected with who you are, the next step is clear: live it.

*Alignment* is where your doing begins to flow from your *being*. It's the practice of showing up with integrity, where your presence, your voice, and your actions all reflect the truth of your *"I am ... "*

In this principle, you explored what it means to lead your life with intention. You discovered that *Alignment* isn't about doing more—it's about doing from a place of wholeness. You let go of the old story that said you have to hustle to prove your worth. Instead, you asked yourself: *What does it look like to move through life in a way that's deeply true?*

In the seventh strategy, *Connect Intentionally*, you began to see that *Alignment* isn't a solo act. It lives in your relationships, too. The people you surround yourself with, those who see, support, and stretch you are part of your *SelfPowerment*. You learned that intentional connection starts with showing up as your full self.

Then, in the eighth and final strategy, *Create Your Future Self*, you were invited to become the woman you're meant to be—on purpose. Not by default or drift, but by design. You learned that manifestation isn't wishful thinking; it's intentional alignment. That each present-moment choice is a powerful step toward who you are becoming.

This principle is the culmination of the *SelfPowerment* journey. You've moved from proving to pausing, from striving to stillness, from resistant to receptive.

Now, you are moving with clarity, courage, and coherence. And as you do, your life becomes not just more successful, but more fulfilled.

## ACTION
Choose one action this week that reflects your future self. It can be bold or quiet, personal or professional—just let it come from the truth of who you are.

## STRATEGIES IN THIS PRINCIPLE
7. Connect Intentionally
8. Create Your Future Self

## AFFIRMATIONS
"I own my presence and voice. I am at ease and aligned."

"I connect with intention to uplift myself and others."

"I am … enough. I choose to live today with purpose and intention, aligned to my human-being."

## PAUSE, REFLECT, REALIGN
- Where in your life are you operating as a human-*doing*—striving, proving, grinding—rather than showing up as a human-*being*, doing from your inner truth and purpose? What would change if you made that inner shift using Alignment as your guide?
- What would it feel like to move through your day in full Alignment, not just driven by tasks but led by who you truly are? Where are you out of sync, and what needs to be realigned?

- As you envision your future self—her presence, voice, and energy—what old limiting belief, noise in your head, or emotions must be released to make space for her becoming *SelfPowered*?
- What's one meaningful way you can bring more integrity and intention into your relationships—so they reflect and support the aligned, evolving version of you?
- What would it feel like to move through your day aligned to your human-being, not just a human-*doing*?

# THE INNER SHIFT

# CHAPTER 22

# Tools for Living *SelfPowered*

"You've always had the power, my dear,
you just had to learn it for yourself."
**~ Glinda the Good Witch**

We've explored the four principles and their strategies. We've read the stories. Now, we have to ask: How do we make *SelfPowerment* a way of living, not just a powerful concept, but a daily reality? What does it mean to bring *SelfPowerment* into the rhythms of your life—with intention, presence, and purpose?

One of the most common questions I receive from women I've mentored is, "Deb, how do I hold on to this? How do I keep 'being centered in who I am' front of mind?"

The answer: by making *SelfPowerment* a habit, by building muscle memory.

Yet because we're all human, we never fully "arrive." We slip into old patterns and encounter new challenges. The good news is that each moment offers a fresh opportunity.

As life continues to unfold and we face new seasons, scenarios, and challenges, *SelfPowerment* becomes a tool we can return to again and again, helping us recalibrate when we need it most.

The more familiar you become with the practice of checking in with yourself—pausing to find stillness, quieting the noise, and accepting the present moment—the more naturally you'll begin to live aligned with your true self as your future unfolds.

Think of this as your "practice space"—where concepts become habits, strategies become strengths, and insight becomes the power to choose differently.

## Tools and Guides to Help You Move Forward

To support you in living *SelfPowered*—moment by moment, choice by choice—this section includes:

- The InnerShift Map, a visual and practical tool to help you locate where your energy is, recognize what's pulling you out of alignment, and gently return you to your center.
- Scenarios that reflect common challenges high-achieving women face, from leadership pivots to burnout recovery, and how to address them with *SelfPowerment* principles.
- More stories of women who, like you, chose to rise, not by doing more, but by becoming more of who they already are.

These tools are not one-size-fits-all. They are invitations to return to yourself, to try again, to make your choice in each present moment.

Let them meet you where you are and guide you toward where you want to go.

After all, the journey is not about becoming someone new; it's about remembering who you've always been.

# CHAPTER 23

# The InnerShift Map: A Guide to Presence and Power

What started as a simple time-and-space chart from my executive coach's book[31] has become something much more: a powerful and transformative tool within the *SelfPowerment* Framework: the InnerShift Map.

Over the years, I've refined and used the map, first in my own transformation, and later as a guide for coaching high-achieving women navigating moments of disconnection, doubt, and emotional overload.

More than a visual or a diagram, this is a tool for reflection, a gentle diagnostic for your inner world. It reveals where your energy and focus have drifted, and most importantly, it points the way back to your center. Back to presence. Back to *"I am ... "* Back to choice.

At the heart of this model is a simple truth: the only place you can access your power is in the present moment.

When you're grounded in the present moment, in your *"I am ... "*, you are no longer reacting from pain, frustration, or anxiety. You are acting from *presence*. This is your zone of clarity, stillness, intention, and aligned choice.

But most of us don't live there consistently. Old stories, cultural pressures, inner doubts, and a fear of the unknown often pull us away.

The InnerShift Map helps us visualize these energetic patterns. And when we can identify where we are, we can make the choices we need to re-set and re-align.

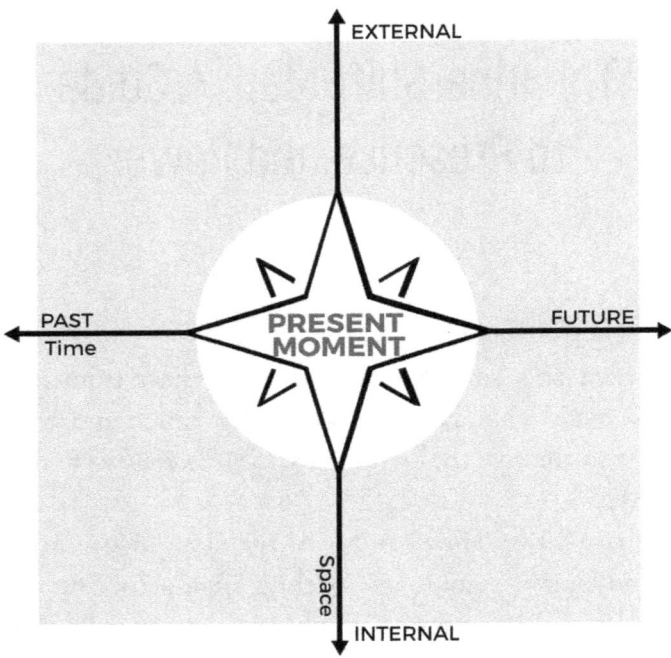

### The Axes of Awareness

The map is divided along two axes: time (left to right) and space (top to bottom).

On the time axis, you have the past on the left and the future on the right.

On the space axis, the top represents the external influences and expectations you deal with, i.e., voices, pressure, systems, cultural expectations, and norms. Those are forces outside your control.

The bottom of the space axis represents the internal influence and pressure you experience, i.e., your inner critic, doubt, ego, and fear. Those are forces you can recognize and control.

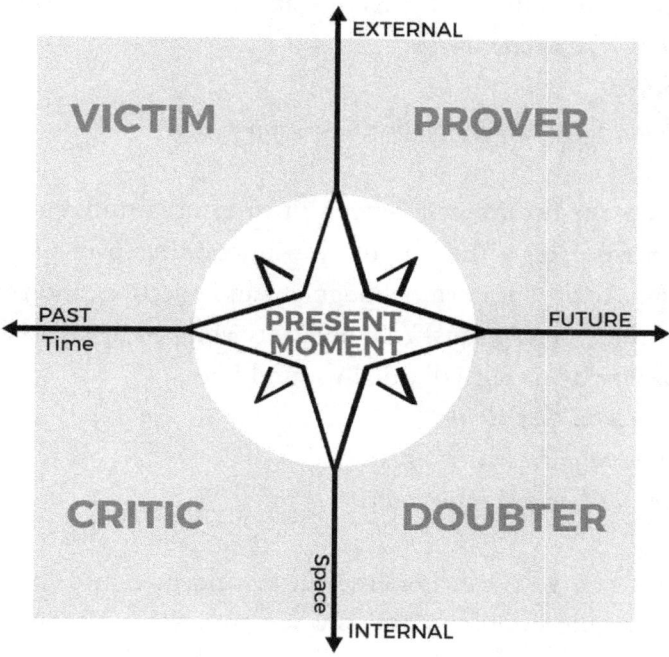

## The Four Quadrants

When you move out of the present moment, your energy gets pulled into one of four quadrants.

Give in to the past and external influences, and you become a victim. This quadrant holds old wounds and echoes of external mistreatment.

Here, you're still carrying the weight of what happened *to* you, letting it shape your confidence, self-worth, and choices today.

**As a victim**, your self-talk might sound like:

- *They didn't support me.*
- *It's not fair.*
- *I cannot believe this happened to me.*

When you're dragged out of the now and give in to the past and internal influences, you become a critic. This quadrant is where guilt, shame, and self-blame live. You're stuck in rumination, playing the same painful loops of past mistakes.

**As a critic**, your inner voice becomes harsh and heavy. It may sound like:
- *I should've known better.*
- *I failed.*
- *I could have prevented this from happening.*

Lean into the future while giving in to external influences, and you become a prover. This is the land of over-functioning, over-preparing, and over-pleasing. You're anticipating judgment and rejection, and you're trying to control others' perceptions. Your energy is wrapped in external approval.

**As a prover**, your self-talk might sound like:
- *What will they think?*
- *I need to prove myself again.*
- *They will never promote me.*

Finally, when you lean into the future and give into internal influences, you become a doubter. This is where imposter syndrome lives. Fear and unworthiness keep you from moving forward. You wait, hesitate, and question yourself, even when you know you're called to act.

**As a doubter**, your self-talk might sound like:
- *I'm not ready.*
- *Who do I think I am?*
- *I cannot do everything required for this role.*

## The Center: Where Presence Becomes Power

While the four quadrants reveal where your energy drains, the center— the present moment—is your power source. It's not neutral ground; *it is sacred space.*

This is where your *"I am ... "* lives. Not in reaction, but in revelation. When you're here:
- Your breath brings you back.
- Your intuition is louder than your doubt.
- Your next right step becomes clear, not from force, but from stillness.

You may only glimpse this space at first. However, with practice, you can learn to return anytime—during a meeting, in a moment of conflict, or while simply going about your day.

This is the heart of the InnerShift: not escaping the quadrants, but noticing when you've been pulled into one, then gently guiding yourself back to center.

## Why This Map Matters: A Real-World Example

Let me share an experience from a woman I am mentoring as part of a mastermind program.

## Diya's Story: Making the Inner Shift

Diya is a high-performing leader navigating a major organizational restructuring. She had just been chosen for a new, undefined role, but instead of feeling excited, she felt immense pressure from every direction. The company was in flux, and while she was aligned with her current boss, stepping into this new opportunity would mean leaving that partnership behind and stepping into the unknown.

Her new boss seemed supportive but vague and unclear about goals thanks to the state of the company's strategic initiatives. Under such open-ended expectations, Diya found herself spinning in self-doubt.

When we walked through the InnerShift Map together, it didn't take her long to notice, "Oh, I'm definitely a *Prover*. I'm trying to win everyone's approval before I even step into my power!"

We traced her energy—how she was projecting into the future, managing everyone else's expectations, and forgetting her own voice.

She was also dipping into the *Doubter*, wondering if she was truly ready. Did she have the skills and talent to succeed in the new role? Even just talking about these insights, Diya's breath became shallow and her body tense.

Noticing, she guided herself into a moment of stillness by taking just a couple of conscious breaths. With her hand on her heart, she softly whispered her *"I am ..."* statements.

Then, with each inhale and exhale, she began to visualize herself shifting—first from the Doubter quadrant to the center, then from the Prover to the center, returning, breath by breath, to her inner being.

I am clear. I am capable. I am at peace.

A big smile appeared on her beautiful face. Her posture shifted. Her energy changed.

"I get it," she said as she looked me in the eyes.

She didn't have to prove anything. She knew she was ready. She just had to return to center, back to herself. Which is when her real inner shift occurred.

\* \* \*

Remember, *SelfPowerment* isn't about perfection. It's about *awareness*. When you're spinning, stuck, or scattered, the InnerShift Map helps you see. And once you see, you can choose.

This map gives language to your emotional geography—and permission to return to presence.

## The Power of Recentering

For many, using the InnerShift Map has become a life-changing practice. It shows you where you've "misplaced" yourself—and how to reclaim her.

Whether you're facing burnout, grief, fear of change, or simply the emotional chaos of everyday life, this model offers a path back to peace. It doesn't erase what's hard. It reminds you that you have a choice.

And that choice always starts in the now.

You can return to your *"I am ..."* at any time: In traffic. In conflict. In transition. Even in heartache. And especially in those sacred, quiet moments when you're finally ready to trust yourself—and trust life— again.

# CHAPTER 24

# Applying *SelfPowerment* in Real-World Situations

A s we all know, challenges are inevitable in the dynamic careers of high-achieving women. But through the *SelfPowerment* Framework, those challenges can become defining moments—opportunities to lead with clarity, stillness, purpose, and intention.

Whether you're preparing for a board presentation, navigating a difficult boss, managing high-stakes decisions, or transitioning into a new role, the principles and strategies offer a grounded, repeatable way to come back to yourself and lead from within.

One of the most powerful ways to internalize these skills is by seeing how others have lived them out in real situations.

As you explored the *SelfPowerment* principles, you followed Alex's journey. While she may not be exactly like you, her experience reflects something familiar in many of us.

Alex was accomplished and respected but often felt disconnected inside. She had followed the path, checked the boxes, and played the part—but somewhere along the way, she lost sight of herself.

Through *SelfPowerment*, she began to see how much of her drive came from a desire to meet others' expectations rather than her own truth. She stopped chasing certainty in someone else's eyes and began returning to her center.

She gave herself permission to *Acknowledge* her human-ness and honor her needs.

She dared to *Awaken* her inner being, embracing stillness, quieting the noise in her head, and reconnecting to purpose.

She learned to *Accept* the moment instead of resisting it—and in doing so, reclaimed her power of choice.

Eventually, she *Aligned* with her deeper vision, her true voice, and her own terms.

Whether Alex earned the title or chose to walk away no longer mattered. She didn't need the role to prove her worth. She had already made the inner shift. She had returned to herself.

This is the heart of *SelfPowerment*.

You don't rise to meet the world's expectations. You rise to meet *yourself*.

And there's nothing more powerful than a woman who chooses to do exactly that.

## Applying the Principles

As you lean into your *SelfPowerment* journey, you'll encounter a wide range of situations. But what does it actually look like to let the principles guide you?

Let's explore three scenarios. While hypothetical, they reflect very real experiences and show how the principles naturally emerge in moments that call for presence, resilience, and aligned action.

As you read, notice how the principles surface in an organic rhythm—meeting you exactly where you are and gently guiding you back to your human-*being*, doing.

Along with it, you'll find real-world accounts of women actively walking out *SelfPowerment*. These aren't polished success stories. They're honest reflections of navigating complexity, pressure, and growth in real time—and the strength and hope that rise when the principles take root.

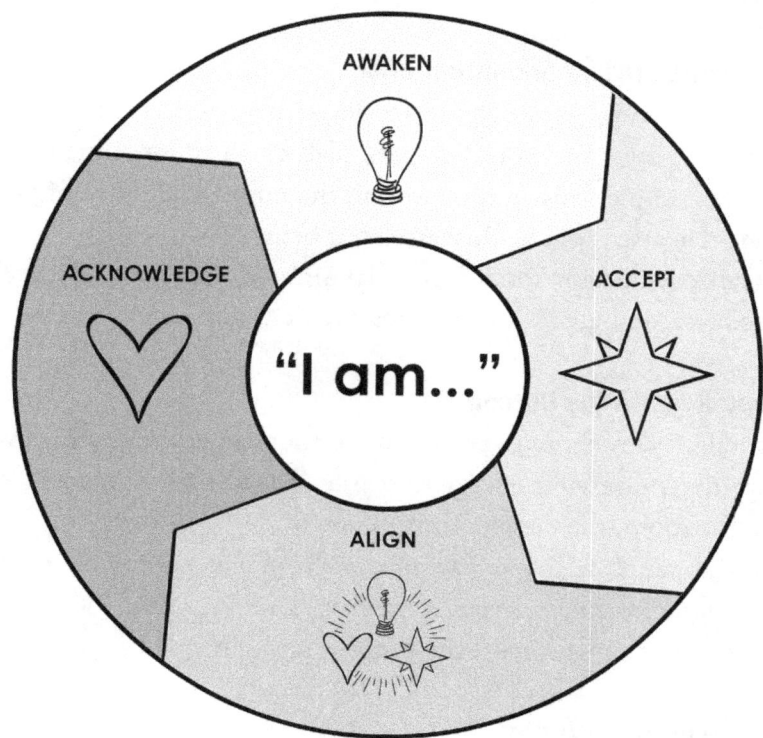

## When Preparing for a Board Meeting or Big Presentation

You're stepping into an environment where visibility, pressure, and leadership intersect. It's more than just slides and data—it's about how you show up, how grounded you are in your truth, and how clearly your presence reflects your power.

### 1. Acknowledge: Step into Your Power

Begin by honoring your strengths. These may include strategic insight, clear communication, financial fluency, and vision. These are more than competencies—they're your superpowers. Revisit a time when you delivered with confidence and clarity. Let that moment anchor you.

Ask yourself: *What strengths will I bring into this room?*

You're not here to prove—you're here to lead. Let your preparation flow from confidence, not fear.

## 2. Awaken: Be Present and Intentional

Before the meeting, create space to quiet the noise. Take a few deep, intentional breaths. Feel your feet grounded on the floor. Tune in to your breath. This simple pause returns you to the now—your zone of power.

Don't rehearse the fear. Rehearse your being.

Visualize yourself: Your energy landing in the room with clarity, groundedness, and grace. You are present, alert, and open.

## 3. Accept: Release the Outcome

It's natural to feel nervous or anticipate tough questions. Acknowledge that. But don't give your energy to stories that haven't happened. Accept what is: the room, the people, the unknowns.

Remind yourself: *This is a business meeting, not a test of my worth. I'm here to communicate with presence, not perfection.*

Accept the moment, trust the process, and stay open to possibility.

## 4. Align: Lead from Within

Ensure your message aligns with the company's greater vision—but more importantly, align it with your voice. Choose a tone and posture that reflect your *SelfPowered* presence.

Is this a moment to lead with visionary energy? Executive calm? Purposeful clarity? Choose with intention.

Ask yourself: *What do I want people to feel when I enter the room? What do I want them to remember when I leave?*

Leverage the relationships and insights around you. Invite support. Lead the room by being in the room—attuned, intentional, and self-led.

## SelfPowerment Reflection

After the presentation or meeting, take a moment—not to analyze, but to acknowledge.

- *What did you learn about yourself?*
- *How did it feel to show up with presence?*
- *Where did you stretch? Where did you stand tall?*

This isn't about one meeting or one presentation. It's about becoming *SelfPowered*.

You're not just *doing*. You *are* the human-*being*, doing.

## Holly's Story: Returning to Self

Holly was a rising star. Brilliant in data and AI, she was crushing it at a global consulting firm. But she was also burning out. The long hours, the blurred boundaries, the perfectionism—it caught up with her.

She made a leap, moving into a director role overseeing an AI and data analytics group at a financial firm. But instead of relief, she found resistance. Outdated systems. A culture averse to change. Isolation. She questioned everything, including herself.

When Holly reached out to me, she was paralyzed by fear and self-doubt. "What if I made the wrong move? What if I have to crawl back to consulting? What if I ruined my entire career with this one decision?"

Together, we paused. We breathed. We reframed. I asked her to revisit old assessments. To reread her performance reviews. To remember her superpowers.

That weekend, she grounded herself in her strengths, her passions, and what alignment would feel like. I also encouraged her to take time for self-care. Her favorites of yoga and running would connect and reset her body, mind, and soul.

She stopped spinning and started seeing clearly. She reached out to her old firm, and they welcomed her back without hesitation.

But Holly didn't return as the same woman. She had spent time in transition rediscovering herself—through yoga, gardening, and journaling. She set new intentions and had a clear purpose. She built boundaries. And she reentered with new energy: grounded, confident, *SelfPowered*.

"Last fall, I felt crushed," she told me. "This time, I feel whole."

That is the gift of *SelfPowerment* in real time.

## When Navigating Workplace Crises or Conflict

Whether you're dealing with a difficult boss, a toxic team dynamic, or an operational crisis that puts everything on the line, these are the moments that push you to your edge. They test your presence, clarity, and power.

They can shake your confidence, cloud your thinking, and pull you away from your center.

But they can also become defining moments—opportunities to return to yourself and choose how you will lead.

### 1. Acknowledge: Reclaim Your Power

Start by recognizing your worth, no matter what is happening around you. You bring unique skills, ideas, and emotional intelligence to your team.

If your boss is undermining you, yelling in meetings, or taking credit for your work, it can feel deeply personal. So, remind yourself: *This is not a reflection of my value.*

Give the situation space without attaching it to your identity. Acknowledge your ability to remain calm under pressure, your crisis management skills, your ability to stay composed.

Document your contributions. Not just to protect yourself, but to stay connected to the truth of your impact.

Your work matters—even when it's not being recognized.

### 2. Awaken: Stay Present and Professional

Conflict and crisis thrive on reaction. Your power lives in response. In difficult conversations or high-pressure moments, come back to your breath.

Ground yourself in the now. Choose to respond from your center rather than reacting from your fear. This isn't about ignoring your emotions—it's about staying centered enough to lead with inner power.

The more reactive the environment becomes, the more anchored you must be. Your stillness is your strength.

### 3. Accept: Release the Illusion of Control

You cannot change your boss's behavior. You cannot prevent every crisis. But you can choose how you show up.

Acceptance is not giving in—it's anchoring in reality.

Accept that the system may be flawed. That someone may be unfair. That the outcome may not be ideal. And then ask: *What is mine to hold?*

When you release what's not yours, you create space to focus on what is—your intentions, your next steps, your integrity.

### 4. Align: Lead with Purpose, Not Emotion

Respond with intention. Align your actions with your role, your values, and the needs of the moment.

In a crisis, stick to the company's plan. But also stay attuned to your voice and the tone you're setting. In conflict, protect your professionalism while also seeking the right allies and support systems. Let your inner voice be stronger than the noise around you.

Choose the *SelfPowered* voice that leads with calm, courage, and purpose.

### SELFPOWERMENT REFLECTION

Remind yourself:

- *Even when things feel out of control, I am not.*
- *Even when someone else is behaving badly, I can rise.*
- *Even when the pressure mounts, I can access stillness.*

Next, ask yourself:

- *What am I being called to own in this moment?*

- *What can I let go of that is not mine to carry?*
- *What would leadership look like if I trusted myself completely?*

You do not need permission to rise. You only need to return to your "*I am …*"

## Jasmine's Story: Rising to the Occasion

For over a year, I had been mentoring Jasmine, Managing Director of U.S. Operations at a global tech company. She's smart, passionate, and determined. But she had been hitting walls.

Her UK-based leadership team felt disconnected. Her immediate supervisor, though aligned in vision, wasn't aligned in strategy, and that difference created constant tension. Resources were blocked. Support was missing. And Jasmine began to doubt whether her voice even mattered.

Then, everything changed. Her boss was suddenly let go. And in that moment, Jasmine had a choice: shrink or rise. She chose to rise.

She prepared with intention. She aligned her message. She knew this was her moment to lead from her center, not to impress, but to express. In a pivotal meeting with the CEO, she laid out her vision with clarity and confidence. Her leadership landed.

The CEO saw her. Promoted her. Gave her a raise. And, more importantly, acknowledged her as a key strategic player.

Jasmine didn't just show up with a PowerPoint. She showed up with *power*. She had awakened to her voice, aligned her actions, and accepted her reality without being defined by it.

"One of my strengths, and maybe my challenge too, is that I'm always open to future possibilities," Jasmine shared. "It's hard for me to pin down exactly what my goals are because they're always shifting. I think in pencil, not pen. I don't want to be boxed in."

Looking up and out with *SelfPowerment* allowed her infinite possibilities to unfold.

## When Leading Through Change, Challenge, and New Chapters

Whether you're stepping into a new leadership role, navigating a major organizational shift, or considering a bold career change, these moments stretch you.

They demand more of your courage, your clarity, and your commitment to yourself. But they also hold the power to transform you.

This is where *SelfPowerment* becomes more than a philosophy—it becomes your way forward.

### 1. Acknowledge: Own Your Superpowers

You are here for a reason. Whether you're leading change, launching something new, or navigating internal upheaval, take time to reconnect with what you bring.

What are your leadership strengths? Your unique gifts? The inner wisdom and lived experience that only you have?

Prioritize your well-being—it's not just self-care, it's strategy.

And if you feel fear or sadness rising, ask: *Is this fear mine—or something I inherited?*

Maybe it's an old narrative: *women don't lead this way.*

Maybe it's generational: security first, even at the cost of joy.

Whatever it is, name it. Then choose to break the cycle. You have the right to feel powerful in your role, confident in your decision-making, and proud of how you show up—even when it's hard.

### 2. Awaken: Begin Within

The first step in any transition is returning to center. Clarity begins in stillness. When faced with uncertainty, learning to catch and release the noise is essential—whether it's fear of leaving a stable job, anxiety over a resistant team, or disorientation in the face of corporate restructuring.

Come back to your breath. Ground yourself in stillness. Feel your being. Feet on the floor. Supported. Present.

You don't need to have all the answers. You just need to reconnect with your why. Why does this role, this pivot, this opportunity matter to me? What future am I being invited to step into?

Self-doubt is just noise. Quiet it. Listen for your inner voice. Tune into your purpose.

## 3. Accept: Let Go, Move Forward

You may not love the change. The team may resist your leadership. You may question if you're ready to leave a paycheck for a passion.

But whatever the moment holds, meet it with honesty and courage. Accept it for what it is. Not because you agree with it, but because resistance steals your power.

Acceptance isn't surrender—it's strategy. It's how you stop wasting energy on what's outside your control and start using that energy to make bold, aligned moves.

Say yes to the financial independence you've earned.

Say yes to decisions that reflect your values.

Say yes to possibility—even if it's not fully clear yet.

## 4. Align: Lead from Your Truth

Whether you're presenting a new vision, pitching your business idea, managing change, or building a culture of trust—your voice matters.

Speak clearly. Speak honestly. Speak intentionally. Surround yourself with people who see your vision. Build the relationships that support your growth.

Communicate with empathy—especially when others feel uncertain or afraid.

And hold yourself accountable—not to perfection, but to integrity.

Align your actions with your *"I am ..."* and lead by example.

Your presence will do the rest.

## SELFPOWERMENT REFLECTION

Ask yourself:

- What part of me is ready to evolve—even if I'm afraid?
- What is the opportunity beneath this change?
- Where can I honor what is and still lead what's next?

Transitions are not detours; they are doorways. You are not starting over; you are stepping deeper into your truth.

The *SelfPowered* path isn't always easy, but it is always yours to choose.

## Cheryl's Story: Letting Go to Move Forward

Cheryl had been an executive at a large global firm for over two decades. Respected, results-driven, and deeply loyal, she especially loved the mentoring and leadership aspects of her role.

But after a leadership restructure brought in executives aligned with the parent company, Cheryl began to feel increasingly sidelined. Her voice no longer carried weight. Her seat at the table disappeared. And then—unexpectedly—so did her role.

"I was blindsided," she told me during one of our first conversations. "This was supposed to be my final company, my legacy role. After everything I gave, it felt like I was just ... erased."

Through our work in the *SelfPowerment* Mastermind and one-on-one mentoring, Cheryl began moving through the four principles.

She started by facing the truth: she wasn't just angry and hurt—her identity had become deeply entangled with her title. "I was always Cheryl-from-somewhere," she said. "Never just Cheryl." The silence that followed her exit felt disorienting but also quietly revealing.

As she moved into *Awakening*, she began to recognize what she had been pushing aside: the fatigue, the constant inner noise, the subtle but persistent misalignment. "I'd been grinding for so long, I didn't even realize I had stopped listening to myself."

Cheryl started letting go—not just of the role, but of the guilt, the proving, and the belief that her worth was defined by her title. She began to reinvest in her health, body, and soul.

Her breakthrough came through *Acceptance*—learning to honor what was, without judgment, and open herself to what could be. In time, she stepped into a short-term role that allowed her to help others and reestablish her voice as a thought leader. It became a bridge, not just professionally, but personally, anchoring her in clarity, authenticity, and wellbeing.

She wasn't starting over—she was starting true. She began leading from wholeness, not obligation. And when she walked into rooms, she no longer felt the need to prove herself. She knew she belonged—in any chair, in any room.

"Once I stopped clinging to what I lost, I could finally see who I was always meant to be," she shared. "Letting go wasn't the end. It was the beginning of becoming who I truly am."

## Choosing What Happens *Through* You

Utilizing the *SelfPowerment* Framework in professional settings empowers women to meet complexity with clarity, pressure with purpose, and challenge with courage.

When we lead from the inside out, we are grounded in awareness, authenticity, and alignment—we stop reacting to what's happening around us and start choosing what happens *through* us.

This framework is more than a tool; it invites an inner shift—a transformation that redefines success not by titles, to-do lists, or other people's expectations, but by fulfillment, intention, and alignment with your human-*being*.

It's a conscious movement from striving to thriving—from external achievement to internal coherence.

Whether it's through the scenarios or Holly, Jasmine, and Cheryl's stories, I hope you've found encouragement and inspiration to use the principles of *SelfPowerment* in your everyday life.

As you reconnect with your truth, you begin to measure success not by how much you do, but by how aligned you are in your doing. Not by how others see you, but by how fully you see and honor yourself.

This approach not only enhances individual performance and presence but also creates ripple effects that inspire teams, elevate culture, and unlock new possibilities for growth.

It equips high-performing women to navigate their careers with power and peace, not by doing more, but by being more fully themselves.

In every meeting, every moment of doubt, every bold next step, the *SelfPowerment* principles are your guide.

They're not only strategies. They're a way of becoming.

You are not just leading. You are transforming.

And the path forward begins with your next aligned choice.

# CHAPTER 25

# New Beginnings

Every morning, I walk the golf course behind my house when it's still early. It's quiet. Still. No meetings, no notifications—just the path stretching ahead to the line of the trees on the horizon, the sound of birds overhead, and the occasional squirrel who seems to know more about pausing in the moment than most executives I've met.

This is where I reset. This is where I remember who I am beneath the layers of roles, decisions, and expectations.

On those walks, I often think about the women I've come across over the years—brilliant, capable, high-achieving women who are holding so much. They're leading teams, solving complex problems, raising families, and doing it all while carrying a quiet, invisible weight.

They've achieved success in multiple ways, yet many still feel fragmented, pulled in too many directions, and quietly searching for something more.

And I wonder: What if more women were living *SelfPowered*—not someday, but now?

Not striving.

Not proving.

Not waiting for permission.

But making choices … with clarity, stillness, and purpose.

The *SelfPowerment* Framework is transforming the lives of women just like you. Women who, even with full calendars and impressive titles, feel the ache of disconnection. Women who dared to say, *There has to be another way.* Women who choose to step into their *"I am …,"* to rewrite their definition of success, and to lead from presence, not pressure.

You may not be standing at a dramatic crossroads. You may not be in crisis or preparing to walk away from something big. But eventually, there will be a moment, and it will come, that asks:

- *Are you aligned?*
- *Are you awake?*
- *Are you willing to return to your center and be true to you?*

When that moment comes, you'll know what to do. Because you've already done something powerful; you've paused long enough to reflect, to remember, and to choose presence. That's not a small act. That's where *SelfPowerment* begins.

You are a human-*being*, first, not merely accomplishing, but unfolding into the next, truer version of yourself. You're not defined by roles or titles, but grounded in presence, purpose, and inner power. The power comes when you are present in the moment; you can make sure that what you *do* never takes precedence over who you *are*.

The clarity you've found, the questions you've asked, and the truths you've remembered are your guideposts. Not only for leading and living, but for *becoming*.

Because when you live in alignment, the inner shift happens.

True power lives in the present. When we quiet the noise, stand still in confidence, and choose from within, our lives begin to align with who we truly are.

We all carry an "Ellis Island story"—our roots, our beginnings, and the beliefs and patterns we've inherited along the way. Some were passed down with love. Others with fear. Some strengthened us. Others held us back.

But legacy is not just what we're given—it's what we choose to pass on. And once again, we have the power to choose.

- To choose to recognize the beliefs that no longer serve us, then gently lay them down.
- To choose to reclaim the parts of ourselves buried under decades of perfectionism, people-pleasing, or pressure.
- To choose to return to wholeness, to freedom, and to the joy of leading as fully ourselves.

I have made choices in my own life again and again. In boardrooms. On morning walks. In seasons of doubt. In seasons of breakthrough. In the middle of ordinary days and extraordinary decisions.

And now, I'm inviting you to do the same.

So, let me ask you: *Why not you?*

You don't need anyone's permission.

You don't need to wait until you feel ready.

The truth is, if you're reading this, you've probably already begun! You've made the courageous choice to start showing up differently—more rooted, more present, more fully yourself.

And that matters.

Because here's the thing: your transformation doesn't end with you.

Every choice you make sends a ripple … into your team, your home, your community.

Which brings us to an even bigger question: *Why not us?*

Yes, we've come a long way in the business world. But let's not ignore what's still true: the game wasn't built for us. The rules of engagement in business were designed by and for men. But we're not here to play someone else's game—we're here to change it.

To lead from within.

To lead as women.

And not just for ourselves, but for those who are watching us, following us, believing because of us.

Whether we like it or not, every choice we make is a signal to our teams, our daughters, our granddaughters, and to the next generations of women wondering: Is it safe to be powerful? Is it possible to work and lead without losing ourselves? Is it possible to have a lasting impact on the world as just one person?

It is.

And you are the proof.

So, let me encourage you. Walk your path with intention. Let your presence lead—calm, clear, centered—before you say a single word. And when doubt inevitably creeps in, as it does for all of us, return to the voice within that already knows the truth: you are enough ... and then some.

You've already accomplished so much. You've built, led, and contributed. You've created something meaningful. But now, you're ready for more—not more hustle, but more depth. More alignment. More peace. And true fulfillment doesn't require you to trade away pieces of yourself.

There are infinite possibilities ahead of you. But everything begins with one commitment:

The commitment to live in the moment, *SelfPowered*.

To be the kind of woman who leads not by force, but with presence. Not through noise, but through grounded clarity. Not by molding herself to fit expectations, but by standing fully in her truth.

Because this isn't just about your career.

This is about your life.

Your legacy.

Your inner shift.

Your power to reshape what your life looks and feels like—not just for yourself, but for every woman who comes after you.

So, take a breath. Get still. And ask yourself, quietly and boldly: *Why not me?*

Then let the conformation rise—not from pressure, but from knowing:

You've got this!

## THE SELFPOWERMENT SELF-ASSESSMENT
# How SelfPowered Are You?

### THE NEXT STEP IN YOUR JOURNEY BEGINS HERE...

✓ You've explored the research.

✓ You've read the stories.

✓ You've walked through the framework.

✓ You've felt the call to shift from human-doing to human-being, doing.

You've come this far—now it's time to turn reflection into action.

## TAKE THE SELFPOWERMENT SELF-ASSESSMENT

It's free, quick, and designed for immediate insight. In just 10 minutes, you'll unlock a snapshot of where you are today—and reveal your path toward greater clarity, alignment, and authentic power.

### WHY TAKE IT?

**Clarity**: See where your current mindset and energy sit within the Framework.

**Insight**: Identify strengths to build on and patterns you may want to shift.

**Action**: Receive next steps to guide your SelfPowerment journey.

## START HERE

Take the SelfPowerment self-assessment today.

www.selfpowerment.com/assessment

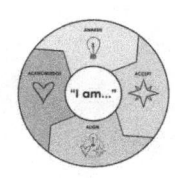

**Because true power isn't about doing more.**
**It's about aligning with who you already are.**

# ACKNOWLEDGMENTS

**To my mom, Alexandra Gima**—your strength, courage, and independence, expressed through your deep family love, relentless drive, and hard work, have been the blueprint of a *SelfPowered* woman. I began with your story, your wisdom, and strength—you were surely ahead of your time and generation. Then I drew from your resilience and authenticity. Your legacy inspires me and your granddaughters every single day. May your memories be eternal through this book and within our family stories, forever and ever.

**To my husband, Mark Smallwood**—your unwavering love, your belief in every part of me, and your steady presence as my greatest supporter and cheerleader have supported me through all seasons of life, both in the highest highs and the deepest dips. Your steadfast nature provides our family with the anchor of love and support. Your love means more than I can say. And now, as "Deb 2.0" with *SelfPowerment,* you continue to stand beside me, prouder than ever. I'm forever grateful for you and the incredible life and journey we share.

**To my dad, Harry Makris**—you left this world far too young, and we have longed for you and your being for the last 50 years. But your spirit left an imprint on my heart and soul. You showed me the world of infinite opportunities from a lens outside of the Greek community in New Hampshire through your relationships and connections in business, community service, as well as local, state, and national politics. Even at a young age, you opened my eyes to what is possible and gave me the permission to begin to challenge the status quo and push forward to new heights.

**To my daughters, Rebecca Saunders and Sarah Gonzalez**—you both are amazingly strong and beautiful. Our deep connection and love bring me incredible joy and a cherished dimension to life as your mother. I am so proud of the *SelfPowered* women you have become: your confidence, your ability to know, accept, and love yourselves in the moment, and your bold, authentic choices for yourselves, your careers, and your families. I will love and cherish you both forever and ever. I promise.

**To my granddaughters, Penny, Stella, and Audrey, and my grandson, Clark**—you have given me the gift of experiencing unconditional love and pure joy all over again. As your *Yiayia*, I see endless potential in each of you. I'm continually inspired by your strength, unique talents, and powerful inner light. I love how you all shine so bright—please never lose that. And remember always to be *SelfPowered* women and yes, Clark, you too, as a *SelfPowered* man.

**To my sister Alexis, my *Yiayia*, my aunties, and my cousin Janis**— thank you for being powerful role models and constant sources of inspiration. You each showed me that there are no limits, no barriers—just opportunities. Through your examples, you helped shape my life and career, and you pointed me toward being *SelfPowered*.

**To my guardian angels and other female ancestors**—you have bestowed upon me the strength and courage to ask, *Why not me?* and whispered in my ear, *You've got this!* helping me to look up and out at a world of infinite possibilities.

**To my executive coaches:**

- **Jim McGovern and Ernie Zissis**—you were both instrumental in helping me rediscover my superpowers and find my voice again. Your support arrived at just the right moment in my professional evolution, and I continue to use the many tools you gifted me.

- **Faye Mandell**—your wisdom and spiritual teachings have been life changing. You helped me understand the power of presence, the meaning of time and space, and how I was beyond just a taskmaster, but a true wise woman, and the importance of loving myself first. Thank you. Your teaching through the key concepts from your book Self-Powerment: The Gateway to a New Way of Living,[32] was the beginning of my inner shift, the nudge I needed to become awakened and aware of my being.

- **Jennifer Buras and Louisa Mattson**—you arrived just when I needed a new spark. You helped me reconnect with my purpose, passions, and inner strengths as I moved into the final year of Strategy Meets Action, through the acquisition, and as I stepped into "Deb 2.0". You lit the idea for this book, you reminded me of my superpowers and my nurturing voice that was buried, and I'm so very grateful for it all.

**To Eckhart Tolle**—your transformative spiritual teachings and the profound wisdom in your books (*The Power of Now*, *A New Earth*, and *Stillness Speaks*) have deeply influenced me. Your voice, first heard in partnership with Oprah's *Super Soul Sunday*, opened my path to deeper awareness and the present moment, egos, and pain bodies. All of the coursework and certification of Becoming a Teacher of Presence continue to guide me into deeper stillness and presence, and to the feeling of peace and joy within.

**To Marissa Buckley** and the **Women of Zen in Zion**—your sisterhood, wisdom, and shared stories have been a treasure. You stood beside me during the early formation of *SelfPowerment* from what started as a journey at this stage of my life and career. You've reinforced my mantras: *Why not me?* and *You've got this*. Thank you for affirming the essence of *SelfPowerment* and being part of this journey.

**To the 52 women leaders and 10 men** I interviewed—thank you for your honesty, your courage, and your willingness to share your stories. Your vulnerability reminded me—and confirmed for many—that we are not alone. You've inspired me beyond words and validated that joy, ease, and peace *can* exist in the workplace.

**To the Magnificent 9**, the inaugural members of the *SelfPowerment* Mastermind Collective—thank you for your trust. Thank you for showing up to the first masterclasses, for testing the exercises and tools, and for courageously sharing your inner wisdom during our one-on-one sessions. Your wisdom and voices are woven into the stories and insights in this book.

**To the many women and men I've worked with** over the course of my career—thank you for inspiring, challenging, and supporting me. You offered opportunities, mentorship, and partnerships that expanded my world and helped me see the limitless possibilities of this incredible journey.

**To Morgan James Publishing** for the partnership in bringing this book to life. Your unique approach to publishing—empowering authors while providing expert guidance—has made this journey both professional and personal. Thank you for believing in this message and for your unwavering commitment to publishing books that make a meaningful impact.

**To Kristen McCall**—your artistry and ability to turn ideas, sketches, and PowerPoint slides into visual storytelling have been magical. Thank you for bringing the imagery of *SelfPowerment* to life with your gift of drawing and creative vision.

**To Adéle Booysen and Tara Cooper**—thank you for your expertise, keen eyes, generous hearts, and brilliant talents of developmental and line editing. You helped bring clarity, emotion, and structure to my manuscript. Your skill and care, as well as your ability to internalize *SelfPowerment*, elevated my story and helped bring out other stories from the research while keeping the message of *SelfPowerment* intact. I'm deeply thankful for all you've contributed to this incredible learning experience.

And finally, **to Karen Anderson**, my guiding light through every step and moment in this entire book journey—thank you for showing me the path forward, expanding my thinking, and helping me uncover and trust in my true voice as an author.

You've been my coach, my publisher, my editor, and, most importantly, my partner through this life-changing process. I marvel at your ability to create magic—whether by deleting one word, moving a paragraph, or helping an idea shine.

You took my draft manuscript and brought forth something extraordinary, a book with vision, power, and polish. Your wisdom, encouragement, and belief in me have meant everything. *"You've got this!"* still echoes in my mind—and yes, Karen, because of you, I do have this. I cannot wait to see where this partnership and journey lead us next.

# ABOUT THE AUTHOR

D eb Smallwood is a transformational leader, speaker, and trailblazer in helping high-achieving women reimagine success on their own terms. Her career spans executive leadership roles at Liberty Mutual, KPMG, TowerGroup (a Mastercard company), and as founder and CEO of Strategy Meets Action— where she earned a reputation for innovation, vision, and impact.

As the creator of *SelfPowerment*, Deb developed a research-based framework that invites women to reconnect with what matters most— with clarity, intention, and purpose. Her work has resonated with high-achieving, high-performing female leaders, women's communities and networks, and executive teams across industries. Combining decades of professional insight with personal experience, Deb's voice is both credible and deeply relatable.

Today, Deb is actively advancing the *SelfPowerment* movement—mentoring executive women, leading impactful mastermind experiences, and engaging audiences through keynotes, podcasts, corporate workshops, and other platforms with tools and insights that inspire meaningful growth and realignment.

Deb lives in New Hampshire with her husband, Mark, loves time with her two *SelfPowered* daughters, and cherishes being *Yiayia* to four beloved grandchildren. You'll often find her on the golf course, at Pilates, taking dance lessons, or walking in nature.

**Curious about what shaped *SelfPowerment* and the framework?**

Download the whitepaper and explore the full research details.

Download FREE bonus materials and connect with Deb at www.selfpowerment.com

Follow Deb at linkedin.com/in/deb-smallwood-06a8034

# ENDNOTES

## Chapter 3

1   www.pewresearch.org/short-reads/2024/02/27/for-womens-history-month-a-look-at-gender-gains-and-gaps-in-the-us/

2   fortune.com/2024/06/04/fortune-500-companies-women-ceos-2024/

3   www.mckinsey.com/featured-insights/diversity-and-inclusion/women-in-the-workplace

## Chapter 8

4   Angelou, Maya. 2008. *Letter to My Daughter*. Random House. 17.

5   Tolle, Eckhart. 2005. *A New Earth: Awakening to Your Life's Purpose*. Viking Press. Paraphrased as frequently summarized in Tolle-inspired teaching and discussions emphasizing the priority of *being* over *doing*.

6   Tolle, Eckhart. "Becoming a Teacher of Presence" workshop, May 2024.

## Chapter 11

7   www.mckinsey.com/featured-insights/diversity-and-inclusion/women-in-the-workplace

## Chapter 12

8   Sandberg, Sheryl and Adam Grant. 2017. *Option B: Facing Adversity, Building Resilience, and Finding Joy*. Knopf.

9   "The Free-Time Gender Gap: How Unpaid Care and Household Labor Reinforces Women's Inequality," Gender Equity Policy Institute, October 2024. thegepi.org/the-free-time-gender-gap/

10 "Standing Up and Stepping In: A Modern Look at Caregivers in the US," Guardian 12th Annual Workplace Benefits Study, Guardian Life Insurance Company of America, 2023. https://www.guardianlife.com/reports/caregiving-in-america

**Chapter 13**

11 Winfrey, Oprah. 2017. *The Wisdom of Sundays: Life-Changing Insights from Super Soul Conversations.* Flatiron Books.

12 Tolle, Eckhart. 2005. *A New Earth: Awakening to Your Life's Purpose.* Viking Press. Emphasis added.

**Chapter 14**

13 Tod, D., Hardy, J., & Oliver, E. J. 2011. "Effects of self-talk: A systematic review." *Perspectives on Psychological Science,* 6(4), 348–356. doi.org/10.1177/1745691611413136.

14 Keng, S. L., Smoski, M. J., & Robins, C. J. 2011. "Effects of mindfulness on psychological health: A review of empirical studies." *Journal of Positive Psychology,* 6(5), 377–388. doi.org/10.1080/17439760.2011.608556.

15 McGreevey, Sue. 2011. "Eight Weeks to a Better Brain." *Harvard Gazette,* January 21. news.harvard.edu/gazette/story/2011/01/eight-weeks-to-a-better-brain/

16 Hölzel, B. K., Carmody, J., Vangel, M., Congleton, C., Yerramsetti, S. M., Gard, T., & Lazar, S. W. 2011. "Mindfulness practice leads to increases in regional brain gray matter density." *Psychiatry Res.* Jan 30;191(1):36–43. doi: 10.1016/j.pscychresns.2010.08.006. Epub 2010 Nov 10. PMID: 21071182; PMCID: PMC3004979.

17 Heiss, Rebecca, "Don't believe in the power of meditation?" @DrRebecaHeiss on YouTube, May 7, 2025. youtube.com/shorts/Nx_DGSQnbVI?si=vv3U-30XchuOLqK6

18 Warner, Jessica. 2021. "Secrets to Surviving Stressful Times." *Scientific American Mind,* Vol. 32 No. 1, January, 14. scientificamerican.com/article/vision-and-breathing-may-be-the-secrets-to-surviving-2020/

19 "How Box Breathing Can Help You Destress," The Cleveland Clinic, August 17, 2021. health.clevelandclinic.org/box-breathing-benefits

## Chapter 15
20 Indra Nooyi interview in *Harvard Business Review*, "What Leaders Eat, Do, Drive, and Cook," February 2017.

## Chapter 16
21 Paraphrase of Gabby Bernstein's teachings in *The Universe Has Your Back* and related talks

## Chapter 18
22 Amelia Earhart, quoted in Goodreads.com via popular quotation collections, original source not easily verifiable
23 Ginni Rometty in *Don't Let Others Define You*, quoted at BrainyQuote. com. Based on her statement reported by Huxley Media.
24 Welch, Suzy. 2009. *10-10-10: A Life-Transforming Decision Tool.* Scribner. Originally published in *O, the Oprah Magazine* and presented at the Nordic Business Forum in 2013.

## Chapter 19
25 Brown, Brené. 2010. *The Gifts of Imperfection: Let Go of Who You Think You're Supposed to Be and Embrace Who You Are.* Hazelden Publishing. 77.

## Chapter 20
26 McKinsey & Company & LeanIn.Org. 2018. *Women in the Workplace 2018.* www.mckinsey.com/featured-insights/diversity-and-inclusion/women-in-the-workplace
27 Wake Forest Professional Development Center. "Networking: A Good Thing for Professionals and Leaders," Inside WFU, Wakeforestuniversity. com, August 28, 2024. inside.wfu.edu/2024/08/networking-a-good-thing-for-professionals-and-leaders/

28  Wolff, H.-G., & Moser, K. 2008. "Effects of networking on career success: A longitudinal study." *Journal of Applied Psychology,* 93(1), 196–206. doi. org/10.1037/0021-9010.93.1.196.

29  No direct source. This paraphrase is based on her broader message in interviews and talks.

## Chapter 21

30  Sheldon, K. M., & Elliot, A. J. 1999. "Goal striving, need satisfaction, and longitudinal well-being: The self-concordance model." *Journal of Personality and Social Psychology,* 76(3), 482–497.

## Chapter 23

31  Mandell, Faye. 2003. *Self-Powerment: The Gateway to a New Way of Living.* Dutton Adults.

## Acknowledgments

32  Ibid.

33  Commonly attributed to Viktor E. Frankl, though not found verbatim in his published works. The quote reflects themes from *Man's Search for Meaning* (Boston: Beacon Press, 2006).

# RESOURCES

As part of my own *SelfPowerment* journey, I've gathered resources that have helped me reconnect with presence, find stillness in transition, and trust the unfolding of life. Whether you need a reset, a deeper dive, or a gentle reminder to quiet the noise, these voices have guided me—and I'm honored to share them with you.

These aren't just books, podcasts, or workshops. They're *anchors*—reminders to return to yourself, to breathe, and to embrace the power of aligned being.

## Books That Restore, Realign, and Reframe

*The Power of Now* by Eckart Tolle
   A spiritual classic that teaches the importance of presence—letting go of past regrets and future worries to fully inhabit the current moment

*A New Earth: Awakening to Your Life's Purpose* by Eckart Tolle
   Explores how ego-based thinking limits our fulfillment and how awakening to a deeper sense of self can lead to greater purpose, contribution, and consciousness—both individually and collectively

*Stillness Speaks* by Eckart Tolle
   A series of meditative reflections that emphasize the silent space within us as the source of wisdom, creativity, and peace

*The Universe Has Your Back: Transform Fear to Faith* by Gabrielle Bernstein

A spiritual guide to letting go of control and trusting in something greater

*The Gifts of Imperfection* by Brené Brown

Embracing vulnerability, authenticity, and the courage to be fully you

*Let Them Theory* by Mel Robbins

A response to the widespread pattern of individuals surrendering their personal power to external circumstances

*Worthy: How to Believe You Are Enough and Transform Your Life* by Jamie Kern Lima

A deep exploration of self-worth, healing, and embracing our full humanity

*Good Power: Leading Positive Change in Our Lives, Work, and World* by Ginni Rometty

A bold redefinition of leadership rooted in purpose and possibility

*Lean In: Women, Work, and the Will to Lead* by Sheryl Sandberg

A powerful lens on women's leadership, ambition, and navigating power

*The Moment of Lift: How Empowering Women Changes the World* by Melinda French Gates

A compelling call to action for women's equity, voice, and leadership

## Podcasts for Reflection and Depth

### *Oprah's Super Soul Sundays*

My go-to is Oprah's many conversations with Eckhart Tolle—I listen to them over and over. Each time, I hear something new—wisdom that lands deeper, not just in my mind, but in my *being*.

Other favorites are Oprah's conversations with Brené Brown, Daniel Pink, and other thought leaders and spiritual teachers—these are grounding and transformational.

### *Oprah's Book Club*

Of special interest is her recent conversation with Eckhart Tolle in January 2025 revisiting his bestseller, *A New Earth: Awakening to Your Life's Purpose.* It's a powerful conversation on how moving beyond ego-based thinking and embracing presence can transform our everyday lives.

## Subscriptions and Courses to Power Your Journey

### *Eckhart Tolle's Teachings and Courses* (www.EckhartTolle.com)

Explore courses and talks on presence, stillness, manifestation, conscious living, and awakening your being. I especially recommend the following programs, based on my personal experiences: "Becoming a Teacher of Presence," "Conscious Manifestation," "The Power of Stillness," and "Meditations for Sleep and Inner Peace."

# A free ebook edition is available with the purchase of this book.

**To claim your free ebook edition:**

1. Visit MorganJamesBOGO.com
2. Sign your name CLEARLY in the space
3. Complete the form and submit a photo of the entire copyright page
4. You or your friend can download the ebook to your preferred device

A **FREE** ebook edition is available for you or a friend with the purchase of this print book.

CLEARLY SIGN YOUR NAME ABOVE

**Instructions to claim your free ebook edition:**
1. Visit MorganJamesBOGO.com
2. Sign your name CLEARLY in the space above
3. Complete the form and submit a photo of this entire page
4. You or your friend can download the ebook to your preferred device

## Print & Digital Together Forever.

Snap a photo

Free ebook

Read anywhere

www.ingramcontent.com/pod-product-compliance
Lightning Source LLC
Jackson TN
JSHW020433120326
99216JS00007B/841

\* 9 7 8 1 6 3 6 9 8 9 9 8 3 \*